T
H
E

T
H
I
N
K

S
P
A
C
E

...to integrate head, heart, hands and home

THE THINK SPACE

A low-stress behavior management technique,
especially for early childhood

Calvin and Carolyn Richert

Foreword by
Jerry Wyckoff, Ph. D.

Take V

Publications
P.O. Box 4490, Overland Park, KS 66204-4490

First Printing: 1996
Second Printing: 2001

Cover and Book Design: Julie Kiracofe
Cover and Book Photography: Camin Richert
Cover and Book Model: Carlea Richert
Text Illustrations: Ryan Richert
Interleaf Logo design: Microsoft Corporation

Printed in the United States of America

ISBN 0-9651971-9-0

LCCN: 96-60311

PUBLISHER'S CATALOGING IN PUBLICATION DATA
(Prepared by Quality Books, Inc.)

Richert, Calvin.
   The think space : a low-stress behavior management technique,
especially for early childhood / Calvin and Carolyn Richert.
      p. cm.
   Includes bibliographical references and index.
   LCCN: 96-60311
   ISBN 0-9651971-9-0

   1. Child rearing. 2. Behavior modification. 3. Parenting. 4.
Early childhood education. I. Richert, Carolyn. II. Title.
HQ770.4.R53 1996   649.1'23
                                    QBI96-20329

Dedicated to

Emily,

our extraordinary

little friend

— and her family—

without whose

"cooperation"

this book

would never

have been

possible!

THE THINK SPACE
Contents

Enhancements
to Help the Think Space Work Better

FOREWORD

I n a never-ending quest for ways to effectively manage the behavior of children, parents have tried many diverse (and usually ineffective) methods. Then along came Time-Out, a comparatively benign way of punishing children for their inappropriate behavior. Time-Out is preferred over spanking by many, for it has been convincingly demonstrated that corporal punishment can lead to violence and can severely damage parent-child relationships. To be effective, corporal punishment requires that it be delivered swiftly and severely, a one-two punch that is not usually possible or even desirable.

Although experts do not generally consider Time-Out to be a punishment, but rather the taking away of potential reinforcement, it is normally used as punishment by parents, day-care providers and teachers. Punishment is defined as an event that follows a behavior and causes that behavior to lessen in frequency or to stop. Time-Out was found to effectively deliver those results.

Using Time-Out to try to punish away inappropriate behavior caused it to become the new quick-and-easy core of discipline. The process of socializing children — the teaching of behavior that will help children to be an integral part of the social order — is of prime importance and is one of the main tasks of parents. Unfortunately, punishment isn't a very good

----

teaching tool since it focuses mainly on stamping out inappropriate behavior rather than building appropriate behavior.

Calvin and Carolyn Richert, however, have moved Time-Out to a new and constructive level. They have taken away the focus on punishment and instead made Time-Out a teaching tool. In the Think Space concept they effectively give power back to the child, a move that may be frightening to many. But if we carefully consider the nature of humans, we realize that we never really have control over another person, large or small. Giving power back to children, if carefully guided, can be a good thing.

The Richerts provide guidance for that transfer of power by suggesting to the child that the Think Space be used to mainly think about positive alternatives. What happens under these conditions borders on the miraculous. When empowered, children can often make behavioral decisions otherwise blocked by the anger engendered through punishment. And through this empowerment, children learn the important skills of problem solving and decision-making.

In addition to the Think Space concept, Calvin and Carolyn suggest that the role of parents and other providers of child care is the same as the role of good managers. Their notion of child management again takes some control away from the adult and gives it back to the child, so that the child feels that he has at least some control of his life. As good managers do, adults can lead and guide the efforts of children rather than control them. Through that leadership, children learn wise decision-making and positive problem solving.

Foreword

The Richerts' Think Space approach to child management provides the quiet but effective structure children need to learn the important skills required in the world of today. And this book explains it all in an easy, understandable and most practical way.

Jerry L. Wyckoff, Ph.D.

Co-author: *Discipline Without Shouting or Spanking,* Simon and Schuster; *How to Discipline Your Six to Twelve Year Old Without Losing Your Mind,* Bantam-Doubleday-Dell; *20 Teachable Virtues,* Perigee.

ACKNOWLEDGMENTS

Our acquaintance with Dr. Jerry Wyckoff and his wife began on the bleachers of Meadowbrook Junior High School in Prairie Village, Kansas. Together we cheered for our two daughters during their initiation into the demands of interscholastic basketball. Little did we imagine that one day we would meet again under totally different circumstances to discuss some emerging child management techniques we were using in our preschool.

Even though we were at first cautious — almost timid — in part because the success we were seeing was almost too good to be true (surely he would find something wrong with our ideas), our apprehensions were quickly relieved. Gratefully, he was both positive and confident, assuring us that what we were discovering would be gladly received by parents of preschoolers and their professional counterparts, child care providers.

Graciously offering his support, Dr. Wyckoff helped us develop our ideas by lending his technical expertise, reviewing our manuscripts and critiquing areas that needed to be brought into focus from a clinical perspective.

However, when considering who it is that we should thank for their parts in this project, after Dr. Wyckoff, the horizon is

----

filled with hundreds of names and faces. While we will name some of the most recent and direct contributors, we are quite aware that, in the grand scheme of things, we have probably been as impacted by indirect and forgotten influences as we have been influenced by those whom we mention here. To all who read this book and recognize the concepts discussed here as something they shared with us, we give you our sincere and heartfelt thanks.

To our proofing editors — Linda Irwin, our technical proof reader; Lynnette Streeter, who critiqued for style; our daughter Cari Allen, who reviewed the manuscript from a future-parent perspective; and Dr. Jerry Wyckoff who critiqued for practical and technical content — we owe our most sincere praise and appreciation.

To the parents and students of our school, who, over the past decade, have patiently field-tested our techniques and have offered their candid evaluations and suggestions, we are eternally grateful.

Let us be sure to remember Emily, the young lady to whom this work is dedicated, for just being her unique self. What a wonderful gift she has brought to school every day for the past 2 1/2 years. It is she who has served us much of the raw material from which we have forged the single most important child management tool we have ever discovered.

A very special acknowledgment must go to Drs. Paul and Cathy Terranova, the parents of Emily to whom this book is dedicated. Were it not for their patient cooperation and honest evaluations through the years, this book would not have seen the light of day.

Acknowledgments

To my family — the people from whom I require the most patience — I submit my most humble appreciation (with apologies) for their undying support and unconditional love:

- To our four children — Carson, Cari, Camin and Carmen — who had no choice but to endure many parental mistakes which we are now attempting to help other people avoid on behalf of their children;

- To our youngest daughter, Carmen, now a college grad, who ably replaced me in the classroom while I worked on this project;

- To my mother whose undying support constantly renews me and keeps me pressing on when energy fades;

- To my wife and partner-in-service, Carolyn, who courageously but graciously dares to challenge my thinking, tempers my attitudes and literally covers my heartless legalism with her heartfelt sensitivity.

Our artistic team is due our sincere and grateful praise for their creativity and insight:

- To Julie Kiracofe, our artistic co-ordinator, we offer our thanks for the graphic enhancement of our work;

- To Ryan Richert, our nephew, whose chapter-ending sketches were chosen from among other contributors for their creative contribution to the spirit of our writing;

- To our daughter, Camin, who applied her photographic talents to the poses we needed to begin each chapter;

- To our photogenic model, Carlea Richert, (we just couldn't resist using our magnetic 3 1/2-year-old granddaughter!) who unwittingly prepared herself for photographic integrity in this project by spending her share of time in the Think Space during the past two years, we give our warmest thanks!

To Dr. Montrose Wolf and Dr. Ed Christophersen, two of the founders of Time-Out as an effective vehicle of behavioral modification for young children, we owe our sincere appreciation. Instead of regarding the ideas of we who work outside the higher academic community as insignificant contributors to the science of behavior management, they graciously support the Think Space as a viable, effective tool for daily use with preschoolers.

Finally, our most important acknowledgment goes to God himself — our Creator, our Divine Master — who has passed the Think Space concept to us through no merit of our own. Nevertheless, herein is the core of a behavioral management system that is remarkably in tune with human nature the way He created it.

Calvin Richert, Co-owner
Kiddie Kampus Preschool/Day Care
Overland Park KS

April 15, 1996

Chapter 1

Once

Upon

a

Child

1

Chapter One

Once Upon a Child
(In search of a better way)

While waiting to be seated at a popular restaurant near our home, my wife and I noticed a young child, about three years old, making a fuss over something at a nearby table. The mother made one attempt to correct the situation. Seeing that her effort was being ignored, the mother did something that we had never seen a parent do in just that way.

Without any apparent emotion, she took the fussing child by the hand, walked right past us toward the entrance of the restaurant and stopped in the air lock between the inside and outside doors. With her back against the wall, she squatted down to the child's level, looked him in the eye and said something like, *"We'll just stay here until you're finished with your fussing."*

With that, she proceeded to watch cars go by, observe the people walking into the restaurant, look at the landscaping just outside the window and study the pictures on the wall.

All the while, the child carried on with *his* business — playing out a rather serious temper tantrum. Gradually, however, as he realized that his fussing was not going to get any further response from his mother, his noises began to diminish until, finally, he was quiet.

When the mother sensed that her son was sufficiently settled, she smiled at him and asked him a question (presumably, something like, *"Are you finished?"*). He nodded, *"Yes."* They hugged. She stood up, took her relaxed, happy child by the hand and returned to their table.

Now seated at our own table, we were able to observe the mother and child with their family who quietly continued their meal until they finally left without further incident.

At the time, we didn't realize how important that episode would become in our lives, but, in retrospect, it was huge.

It was a classic "teachable moment" for us, and here's why.

ENTER EMILY . . .

On Monday of that week, we had received a new student into our preschool. At 18 months, Emily was already one of those students who makes her mark wherever she goes. Since her older sister had been with us for some time before Emily's arrival, we had been seeing Emily as an infant. From the start, we knew she was exceptional. Early on, she would study us with piercing eyes as if she were trying to figure us out. She would rarely smile (quite the opposite of her congenial older sister), and soon began to display a generally contrary attitude about much of what entered her life. But these sharp contrasts were not because she lacked intelligence. Far from it. She was and is among the most mentally gifted of all the students ever enrolled in our school!

At the very least, this child was a surprise to her parents, both intelligent, caring Ph.D physicists, who had experienced a normal, happy life with their first child. Now their quality of life was being invaded by new and unwanted stresses. They weren't sure how to handle the situation, so they looked to us for help. We were supposed to be the experts!

BACK TO THE RESTAURANT

As we watched the wise mother apply her child management technique, my mind quickly went to Emily.

"How do you think that approach would work with Emily?" I asked my wife.

"I don't know, but we could try it," she responded with a wry smile and a twinkle in her eye.

So we did . . . and it worked!

It wasn't that this approach was entirely new to our thinking, for we had already been doing something along this line. But, more than anyone else, Emily helped us to formalize the idea into a usable, teachable technique. For that we are forever grateful. Thus, the dedication of this book to Emily!

A FRESH APPROACH EMERGES

Gradually, as we applied the idea to other children, refinements were adopted and a name emerged. Research and consultation with respected child psychologists confirmed that we were on a safe track. We began sharing our findings, first with parents and later with other child care professionals. Soon we began to receive invitations to offer these ideas in more formal ways.

While presenting these and other practical child management tools in a workshop called *Discipline Without Damage*, we were repeatedly encouraged to put our ideas into writing without delay, especially the behavior management technique now dubbed the "THINK SPACE".

As is the case with any development of this type, it was not a sudden idea; nor can we credit a single source for our inspiration, although the restaurant story and the entrance of Emily into our lives certainly were pivotal. More realistically, however, the technique which we present here is the result of 28 years of parenting four normally energetic and creative children, 28 years of professional work with other people's children and as many years of reading and research. Add the observation of countless behavioral scenarios, *all* of which worked in some way, either to the advantage of the child, or to the advantage of the supervising adult, and sometimes (if only rarely) to the benefit of BOTH the child and the supervising adult.

SEARCHING FOR WIN-WIN SITUATIONS

It is that last category which is the focus of this book — finding ways to manage children that end up as WIN-WIN situations. The goal is to create outcomes in which both the children and the adults involved in their lives win on some level!

As young parents, we found ourselves using discipline techniques similar to those of our parents and their parents before them. We were determined to do at least as good a job with our kids as our parents had done with their kids! No one needed to teach us (so we thought). We had learned well from our parents!

HOWEVER . . . the day came when, due to unexpected changes in my employment, I joined my wife, Carolyn, in the preschool which we had purchased for *her*, never guessing that one day I would join her in that classroom!

THE WORST DAY AND THE BEST DAY

The day I entered an environment in which my tried-and-true physically-oriented discipline techniques were no longer acceptable, was the *worst* day and the *best* day of my life!

That day was the *worst* because I came to realize that, in spite of surviving life with four kids (all of whom were experiencing above-average success in their various fields of interest), I could no longer use many of the physical "incentives" which I had relied on as a young parent, and later as the principal of a private school which I had helped to start. With those techniques removed, I saw myself as nearly "bankrupt" in my ability to motivate young children to do what I wanted them to do!

(The painful truth was that I did not actually get creative about communicating with young children, until the physically-oriented methods that I thought had served me well, were no longer options!)

It was the *best* day because I was forced to learn to communicate with children on a level almost unknown to me, hard as it was to admit it. (A very tell-tale symptom of the stress I was experiencing was the giant headache I had generated by noon every day for the first two weeks in my new environment!)

I wanted desperately to figure out how to effectively communicate with those little guys and gals. It was a resolve that eventually led us to some ideas that would completely revise the way we view children and how we work with them.

The net result is that we now approach child management with a relaxed confidence which is surprisingly free of stress. In fact, we have come to call the system "LowStress Child Management"[1] for, when practiced properly, stress is drastically reduced for both child and adult.

"AHHH . . . RELIEF AT LAST!"

One midsummer day, while overhearing Carolyn's end of a phone conversation with one of our classroom substitutes, a particular dynamic in this approach surfaced that should be emphasized here.

While we were away for a few days of rest, Betty was having a lot of trouble with Jackson, an unusually energetic and sometimes abrasive four-year-old.

"I've had him in the Think Space six times today already (it was only 10 a.m.), and he just isn't getting any better!" she was complaining on the phone.

Stop right there!

Is the Think Space for Jackson or is it for Betty?

Yes . . . to both questions!

In this case, Betty is discouraged because she isn't getting the results that she would like to see in Jackson. Does that mean that the Think Space isn't working? For the moment, let's assume the Think Space is doing nothing at all for Jackson today. Does that mean that the Think Space isn't working?

No, it doesn't; because, even though Jackson isn't seeming to be influenced by his time in the Think Space, it is still giving Betty a safe alternative for dealing with her frustration — Jackson!

The reality is that there are times when we allow certain children, be they our own or someone else's, to drive us right to the edge of losing control of ourselves. At those moments, whatever action we take is for our own coping and only indirectly for the child's benefit.

In those instances, the Think Space becomes a place to deposit our stresses and frustrations as an option among other less acceptable alternatives.[2]

IT'S ALL IN <u>HOW</u> YOU DO IT!

As for the technique, like anything else, it can be beneficially used and seriously abused. The purpose of this book is to help its readers understand the usefulness of this technique, while teaching HOW to apply the technique so that both child and adult get to the other side of a given issue with patience, respect and task fulfillment all intact!

If your own emotional control with young children is *ever* an issue with you, let us show you a way to handle even the most difficult child without so much as a raised voice, a moment of scolding or a harsh look. Impossible, you say? In the past, I would not have believed that unruly behavior could be handled so peacefully. Gratefully, "the anvil of experience" has given us a tool which has proved to be the single most effective strategy that we have ever used for managing unacceptable behavior! And it works nearly all the time! Too good to be true? Not at all, for we see it work every day. In fact, we have seen the stress level of parenting and of professional child care reduced by half . . . at least!

ASKING VS. TELLING

In a nutshell, the spirit of this whole approach is the difference between *asking* a child to do something and *telling* him to do the same thing. As busy, often preoccupied adults, we frequently take what appears to be the most efficient course of action for getting something done.

- *"Bobby, pick up the toys."*
- *"Jamie, turn off the TV."*
- *"Stevie, get your hands off your brother."*

As commands, each of these orders meets the tests of directness and positive communication. So, what could be wrong with them?

For starters, where is courtesy in those commands? Shouldn't the adult treat the child with the same courtesy he or she would want for himself?

- *"Bobby, please pick up the toys."*
- *"Jamie, please turn off the TV."*
- *"Stevie, would you please keep your hands off your brother?"*

The difference between *asking* and *telling* is most easily revealed in the follow-up to those commands: when the *teller* follows up, he says to the child, *"What did I tell you to do?"* while the *asker* says, *"What did I ask you to do?"*

You ask, *"What difference does any of this make?"*

The difference is so important that we really need to talk about it. We want to help you see that the difference is actually a difference in attitude. We want you to see that the *asking* mind-set is more humane — and in the long run, more productive

----

— than the *telling* mind set. The result — the kinds of behavior you want to see in your child.

Every time you *tell* a child to do something, you invite a contest. Every time you *ask* a child to do something, you invite a voluntary kind of response. The bottom line — *asking* is much more likely to develop a child's inner control while *telling* is likely to encourage rebellion, disrespect and deviousness.

MANAGERS VS. CONTROLLERS

Before concluding these introductory remarks, we need to emphasize that the Think Space is more about *management* and less about *control.*

Throughout this book, "to manage" means
**to rearrange that which already exists
to bring about a desired result that does not yet exist;
to regroup or to reframe
the stuff of which life is composed
into a productive order.**

———————

Other terms that further describe
the spirit of the Think Space:
to lead, to guide, to facilitate.

So, what is the difference between managing and controlling?

All people, including children, need to be *respected.* Most people, including children, instinctively feel *disrespected* when they feel controlled. Furthermore, most people, especially children who are inherently strong-willed, *resist* external control, and are more likely to *challenge* the other person's control than they are to *conform* to it!

In the end, the controller *creates* more problems for himself than he *solves* because he is "swimming upstream" against the flow of human nature, not to mention his belittlement of human dignity!

The *manager* begins by accepting disruptive or other unacceptable behavior as having some teaching value. The *controller* tends to deny that such behavior has teaching value and tries to squelch it or to make it go away — immediately, if not sooner.

Both the *controller* and the *manager* want the children under their care to learn how to handle life, but use two very different approaches. The *controller* thinks that the child will learn best if he does as the *controller* says, thereby placing *himself* at the center of the learning process. The *manager*, on the other hand, helps the child learn, through personal experience, how to handle life and its problems, thereby placing *experience* at the center of the learning process. (Obviously, there are some things that we definitely do NOT want a child to experience, but those are only a tiny fraction of everything a child learns, especially in the first five years.)

"THE DIFFERENCE . . . IS SUBSTANTIAL!"

In the short term, the outcomes of the two approaches may look similar, but in the long term the difference between the two approaches is substantial.

- The *controller* ultimately develops people who FOLLOW while the *manager* develops people who LEAD.

- The *controller* teaches people to use HIS judgment while the *manager* teaches people to develop and trust their OWN judgment.

- The *controller* teaches people that HE can best solve their problems, while the *manager* teaches people to solve their OWN problems.

- The *controller* teaches DEPENDENCE while the *manager* teaches INDEPENDENCE.

Ironically, the Think Space can be a useful tool for both the behavior *manager* and the behavior *controller*. However, more than any other behavior management tool in our experience, this one offers built-in factors which slant it toward the behavior *manager* model and away from the behavior *controller*, especially when applied as described in the chapters that follow.

Finally, since we want this book to be a very practical tool, we have constructed it in a user-friendly format. The early part of the book will be very pragmatic. After an opening story and a brief outline, we offer some basic procedures for applying the Think Space technique. Then, for a more detailed view of this process, Chapter 6 — WHY the Think Space Works — will take you into more technical background information. Chapter 7 challenges us to apply the joyful lifestyle of children to our own lives and offers practical insight to a nearly-ignored part of life when it comes to managing children — the miracle of believing!

THE "FROSTING ON THE CAKE"

The last section, Enhancements, is a collection of key ideas that help ensure success in the use of the Think Space. We have separated these ideas from the main text, not because they are of less importance, but to help you focus on the main ideas as they are being presented. In truth, the Enhancements are just as important as the earlier chapters of this book. They are to the Think Space what tires are to a car — both are essential. For that reason we ask that you give every Enhancement the same quality of attention that you give the first part of this text.

Now, let's open the door to that wonderful new place — the THINK SPACE!

FOOTNOTES

1 *LowStress Child Management:* an innovative child management system which is being detailed in this and other books. Watch for *Discipline Without Damage* and *LowStress Child Management,* both in process at the first printing of this book.

2 See Enhancement B, *Transferring Stress to the Think Space.*

Chapter 2

The

Basic

Idea

2

Chapter Two

The Basic Idea
(A classic story about Joshua and Jeffrey)

Three-year-old Joshua has been a model child . . . until now. It seems that Joshua has just toppled a very nice Lincoln Log cabin painstakingly constructed by five-year-old Jeffrey. In a refreshing moment of propriety, Jeffrey seems to have used all the right responses.

"So, Jeffrey," I ask, "what did you do to Joshua?"

"Nothing."

"Did you talk to him before you told me?"

"Yes."

"What did he say?"

"He wouldn't talk."

"So, what did you do?"

"I came to tell you about it."

"Is that all?"

"Yes."

"Okay. Thanks, Jeff. I'll see what I can do. Would you please wait here?"

"Okay."

"Joshua," I call carefully.

(You see, Joshua is an adopted Honduran child who recently came to us through his adoptive American parents. Since he has never been "in trouble" before, there is a chance he just isn't understanding the language or the rules — or something.)

"Would you come here, please?"

"NO!" he responds curtly.

"Joshua. Did you kick Jeffrey's house down?"

"Yes."

"Was that a mistake?"

"NO."

"Are you ready to help him build his house again?"

"NO."

(I still want to believe that he is only stumbling over the English language, but I am having to admit that we may be seeing the non-compliant — otherwise known as rebellious — streak that his mother had warned us about!)

"Joshua."

"What?"

"Do you need to spend some time in the Think Space?"

"No, no, no." He begins to cry.

"Oh, Joshua. I see that you DO need some time to think about this."

"No, no, no," he wails. "I don't WANT to go to the Think Space!"

(He resists by falling to the floor.)

"Oh, that's all right, Joshua. You don't need to WANT to go to the Think Space. You only need to cooperate."

He doesn't quite know how to respond to that proposition, so I say, "Let's go now, Joshua."

I calmly pick Joshua up, still kicking and screaming, and carry him to the Think Space which, for the time being, has become the "Cry Space."

I gently lay him down on the carpet. He is still kicking and screaming. I am not at all upset with the situation, for I know that I have a graceful way to handle this moment. I know in my heart that all three of us — Joshua, Jeffrey and I — will come through this exercise without the slightest hint of physical or emotional harm.

Although he is still crying, I say, "Joshua, when you are finished with this behavior, we will talk with Jeffrey."

I calmly walk away to do something else. I direct Jeffrey back to the classroom to play, except to leave his broken Lincoln Log house alone.

Soon Joshua is finished crying. I help him stand up, which he does without objection. Hoping he is ready, I ask, "Are you ready to talk?"

"NO!"

"Okay, that's fine. We can wait until you're ready."

Presently, the phone rings. After finishing a short conversation, I ask again, "Are you ready to talk?"

"No." But this time he is not so defiant.

"Fine."

The phone rings again. While I talk, I notice Joshua go to the door of the classroom and then call Jeffrey to come. Jeffrey comes. Joshua says something to Jeffrey. Jeffrey comes to my side . . . waits until I'm finished with the phone.

"Joshua's ready to talk, Cal."

"Good. Okay, Joshua. Did you kick Jeffrey's house down?"

"Yes."

"Was that a wrong thing to do?"

"Yes."

"What can you do to help Jeffrey feel better?"

"Say sorry."

"Okay, go ahead."

"I'm sorry."

"Tell him 'sorry' for what?" I prompt.

"I'm sorry for kicking down your house," he admits to Jeffrey.

"Thank you," Jeffrey responds politely.

"Is there anything else you can do to help Jeffrey feel better?" I continue.

"I don't know."

(I am trying to get him to offer to help rebuild Jeffrey's house, but it isn't working.)

"How about helping him fix his house?"

"Oh yeah. Let's go, Jeffrey."

Joshua happily takes Jeffrey's hand, bounces down the two steps into the classroom and skips over to the collapsed house.

This story so beautifully illustrates the basic idea of the Think Space because it offers such a sharp contrast between a child's being caught in a web of belligerent behavior and his total release from that web without the child being forced or damaged in any way.

In addition, did you notice the numerous forks in the road where we could easily have turned to other traditional — but infinitely less effective — methods, such as scolding, intimidation, coaxing, direct commands, spanking, etc.?

The point *is* that Joshua experienced a 180° turnaround in both attitude and behavior without any coaxing, scolding or other overbearing adult initiatives. The story is a classic illustration of "discipline without damage." Furthermore, since neither Jeffrey nor I "stressed out" over the situation, even the stress which Joshua experienced was short-lived and was totally eclipsed by the joy of his restored relationship with Jeffrey. It was a prime illustration of LowStress Child Management!

Chapter 3

Exactly What IS This Think Space?

3

Chapter Three

Exactly What IS This "Think Space"?

(The Think Space defined and WHEN to use it)

If Noah Webster had known about the Think Space, he might have made an entry in his dictionary something like this:

> **Think Space**
>
> 1. A specific place set apart from the normal activities of life, especially for thinking about future behavior.
>
> 2. A place which separates a person from inappropriate behavior in another location.
>
> 3. A place to "finish" or "drain" (express until completed) inappropriate behaviors and/or attitudes without influencing or hurting other persons.
>
> 4. A place to recover from a state of emotional upset, or to regain emotional balance.

The Think Space

Surely you have heard the shopping parent who frantically tries to quiet her screaming three-year-old when he can't have the toy he wants with,

"Here, Timmy. Have a piece of candy."

Or, as Amy throws herself on the floor, kicking and wailing in a major league temper tantrum, you hear the care provider valiantly trying to reason with her through the noise.

"Now, come on, Amy. You know this isn't going to get you anywhere." (Oh, really?)

Maybe you find yourself warning your unruly four-year-old the third time, the fourth time, the fifth time that, if he doesn't stop pestering his sister, he's *"really going to get it!"*

In each case (and hundreds more unlisted), there is a very simple way to handle the situation. The child needs some space — thinking space.

Here's the idea. Roughly paraphrased, Dr. Ed Christophersen, a well-known child psychologist, would say,

"Why don't you give a kid the dignity that you would want given to you? When you get all confused or upset about something, what do you often need the most? Time and space without any interference. Right? Then, why not give your children the same consideration? After all, they are people too, you know!" [1]

Simply stated, we have found that, when given time to think after exercising some inappropriate or irresponsible behavior, almost all children will adjust their attitudes *and* their behavior without scolding or punishment, and usually very quickly.

In fact, the sad reality is that scolding and punishment will more likely *encourage* the repeating of an undesirable behavior than to have done nothing at all!

Now, quickly let us assure you that we are definitely NOT advocating a passive, do-nothing approach to child management. Far from it. In fact, the mission of this book is to promote positive, but sensitive activism — to show a way of responding to the errant behavior of young children that is far more likely to bring about the desired change than any other form of response that we have ever encountered or experienced.

THE NEW EQ

We are about to share with you our simple formula for success with the Think Space. But, before we do that, we simply *must* stop briefly to recognize some significant research which has recently been published[2] that emphasizes the timeliness of this book. That new research, named EQ for Emotional Quotient, solidly links "emotional intelligence" to a person's overall success in life, especially when it comes to relationships with people. Far from being just a cute take-off on the IQ (Intelligence Quotient) factor, this new research convincingly shows:

- That a person's EQ has a direct effect on his ability to learn; in fact, his EQ may have more influence on his ability to learn than his IQ;

- That a person's EQ is largely set during his preschool years and follows him through the rest of his life;

- That the development of EQ is affected by a child's environment, especially by what he sees modeled by adults (parents and care providers) during his early years;

- That EQ can be boosted through exercises which, among other things, require various kinds of self-control (called inner control in this book).

Here's the kicker . . . the Think Space provides the perfect link between our children and the new EQ research. Why? Because it, like no other behavior management tool that we know of for early childhood, when properly used, encourages the development of emotional maturity in a child. In that light, do you see how important it is that you, as a parent or child-care provider, make every effort to thoroughly learn the Think Space technique and to integrate it into your child's training?

Now, here is our simple formula for success:

Separation + Diffusion + Resolution = Adjustment

SEPARATION

- the act of calmly but firmly removing a child from the environment in which he is using[3] unacceptable behavior.

Six-year-old Robbie was a summer regular in our school, normally good-natured and cooperative, but occasionally obstinate, especially about eating peas. One hot summer day when Robbie was asked to try even the smallest little piece of just one pea on his plate, he "dug in his heels" and *absolutely* would not negotiate . . . at all! (Our practice is to ask the child to try the smallest little piece and *"tell me what you think."*)

Determined to find a way through this impasse, a novel idea hit me. *"What would happen if we would go for a little walk?"* I wondered.

Chapter 3: Exactly What IS This Think Space?

"Good idea," I congratulated myself, and proceeded to invite him for a walk out in the yard. To my surprise, he quickly accepted the invitation, presumably to get out of eating peas.

As we walked, we talked about trees in the yard, birds flying overhead and cars passing by on the street. After a couple of laps around the yard (a total of about 4 minutes), while making our way back to the house, I cheerfully asked him about trying his peas again. He paused for several seconds. I waited with bated breath.

"Okay," he chirped happily, and that was that. He ate a few peas without a hint of resistance. The change was permanent. He never again objected to eating a few of those little green gremlins!

I learned something that day that explains much of the gridlock between children and their parents and providers. Here it is in a nutshell:

A child is territorial by nature. He can quickly "take possession" of any given location as his own, especially when he makes an "emotional deposit" there with some form of abnormal behavior. He instinctively knows that, since the behavior he has chosen is not something his supervising adult wants, he is able to make his own unique deposit on that spot. In his mind, he now owns that spot!

So, what's the solution? Very simply, remove him from that spot. Even if you don't take him from the general area, just moving him to another place in the room or yard may help him to assume a totally cooperative attitude.

DIFFUSION

- disempowering unacceptable behavior by allowing a child to express that behavior in a designated space until he is "finished," or simply taking a child to that space to think about better choices in the future.

A public service radio promotion called "The Family Matters," aired in the Kansas City area, features a series of short sound clips of a mother who is commenting on her method of working through problems at home with her son. It goes something like this:

"When we have a conflict between us, I ask my son to go to his room or somewhere else where he can think about whatever it is that went wrong and how to make it right . . . I want him to grow up to be a thinking person, not just someone who follows someone else's directions, even if that someone else is me!" [4]

Exactly the point. Give the child time and space, and he may very well come to the same conclusion as you. The main difference may simply be that you have had more *time* to come to your conclusion than he has had!

Now, another dynamic that eludes most of us: there is value even in behavior that is deemed by us as unacceptable, behavior that may be more experimental than malicious.

While the primary mission of any given misbehavior by a child is to get a response from the person affected by that behavior, there may be an important secondary mission in the therapeutic value of the activity itself. The child may *need* to cry, or pound, or pout, or scream. Who's to say, *"There's no reason to cry,"* when the child is crying, even if the crying is just to equalize unseen stresses within himself? Or, to demand that the child stop pounding when the child may actually be learning something about noise. Or, to insist that screaming is categorically "wrong" when the child may be experimenting with self-assertion?

Isn't it far better to give the child a place to drain that behavior without guilt or intimidation than to insist that it stop *right now*, only to have it erupt later with even more intensity? Our experience certainly supports that notion, and is firmly reinforced by the scientific research of the psychological and psychiatric communities.

RESOLUTION

- guided, peaceful resolution of conflict, whether only personal (pouting) or involving others (fighting).

Almost every misbehavior includes an offense to some other person, either child or adult. Since children are egocentric by nature (which is essential to their survival, especially during their infancy), they have to be taught that the other people in the world also have feelings. The lack of that sense leads them into all manner of behavior that others find offensive. Therefore, it is the task of both parent and provider to help the child practice treating others the way they would want to be treated.

A vital part of the correction process, then, is to conclude time in the Think Space with some kind of reconciliation — activity that makes the other person *"feel better"* — saying *"sorry for . . . ,"* hugging, helping fix something they messed up, spending play time with the offended person, etc.

ADJUSTMENT

- in recognition of the fact that human nature changes slowly, each correction, at best, is only a fractional portion of a total adjustment.

"How many times have I told you to keep your hands to yourself, Andrew?"

Do you hear yourself in those words? Probably. Why? Because we have a hard time accepting the fact (not merely a theory) that change comes very slowly to human nature. We want to believe that *our* kids should be different — that we shouldn't have to say the same thing "fifty million times" and still seem to be ignored! But, the reality is that your kids are human and that means that they will probably *need* fifty million repetitions to change any given habit, just like all the other human kids in your neighborhood, not to mention yourself!

While much more is coming that will further define our subject, let's finish this section with this definition — brief, simple, to-the-point.

Think Space

A behavioral management technique, especially for young children, comprised of three primary elements
— separation, diffusion and resolution —
to help a child make appropriate adjustments
in relating to himself and his environment.

Now, before you start applying the Think Space to real life, let's discuss the general situations to which the Think Space can be successfully applied and when to avoid using the Think Space.

WHEN <u>TO</u> USE THE THINK SPACE

When an attitude adjustment is needed.

Alice has to wait her turn to paint, so she pouts. Have her "finish" pouting in the Think Space.

When a child is locked into disruptive or other inappropriate behavior.

Christopher has extra energy this morning and is having a hard time remembering to use his "inside voice." He spends time in the Think Space to think about using his inside voice inside and his outside voice outside.

When a child is engaged in conflict with another person or persons.

Trent has just hit Andrew for not letting him play with his Batman car. Trent needs to spend time in the Think Space to think of a better way to encourage Andrew to share his toy.

When a child refuses or resists doing something that he should be doing.

Carlea is putting a puzzle together just a bit beyond her ability, so she is being helped by her daddy. Suddenly, she refuses to pick up even one more piece. She is calmly taken to the Think Space and is told that she may return when she is ready to continue working on the puzzle.

The Think Space

When a child is engaged in a behavior which will be okay to "finish" outside the social environment from which he is being removed.

Libby throws a tantrum when she is asked to pick up the pegs that she just dumped on the floor. She is calmly carried to the Think Space and is told that she may continue picking up the pegs after she has "finished" her crying.

When a parent or provider needs relief from a particular child's abrasive or uncontrolled behavior!

It's Monday morning and the moon is full. Jackson is a problem looking for a place to happen! If left to his own devices, he would have the place in shambles and half the kids hurt. What is Betty to do? Get him to do his own "reality checks" by taking him repeatedly to the Think Space, but each time as if it is the first time that day.

WHEN TO **NOT** USE THE THINK SPACE

When you want to (or think you need to) punish a child.

If you think punishment is really necessary, use some other method, but strictly avoid using the Think Space for that purpose!

When you are too busy, too tired or too lazy to use the Think Space properly.

The Think Space is a tool reserved for those who pursue excellence in child management. Always respect it by using it properly. Avoid mixing laziness and the Think Space as diligently as you avoid mixing drinking and driving!

When your patience is gone.

The only way your patience can be gone is for you to have failed to properly use the Think Space and other behavior management tools at your disposal. The Think Space may, in fact, be your best option, but, first, collect your patience wherever you lost it and start over! Be aware that applying the Think Space *impatiently* will only make matters worse, guaranteed!

When you are too angry or too tired to be rational.

Anger and tiredness are absolutely alike in this respect: they both seriously reduce one's ability to act rationally. The Think Space will help you to keep your cool, but it is not designed to be used as emotional "first aid"!

When you have no other options — the "last resort" syndrome.

The Think Space is such an important tool that it truly resents being saved until all else has failed. In fact, it will probably refuse to work for you as a last resort simply because you may not be able to take the time to intentionally follow proven procedures, an essential element in making the Think Space work.

When it is your only behavior management method.

It is safe to say that the quickest way to make any good child management method a bad one is to make that method your only method! Use the Think Space as you would use seasoning in your cooking. A little improves your meal's taste, but too much will ruin both the food *and* the good reputation of the seasoning.

When the child is beyond rationality — in a delirious emotional state.

An extended emotional outburst can cause a child to completely lose rationality. In fact, a child can become delirious with emotion, at which point it is better to walk away from the situation and let someone else intervene. Your continuing insistence that the child do whatever it is you are asking will only make matters worse. Furthermore, since the child is already irrational, she may not even recall the incident later, a factor in your favor. Just drop the matter for now. You'll have another chance soon!

Chapter 3: Exactly What IS This Think Space?

When you feel like retaliating for the child's wrongs.

Retaliation, whether conscious or unconscious, is an ugly emotion. It can only destroy. Let the child's inappropriate deeds bring their own consequences. Hold yourself above inventing "get even" tactics. In fact, it is impossible to "get even," for when you stoop that low, the scales always tip against you. This is absolutely true!

For more thoughts about the correct use of the Think Space, please refer to Enhancement A, titled *"Cautions."*

Finally, since "recycling" has become such a familiar idea, let's think of the Think Space as a place where a child's misbehavior is "recycled" into building blocks for future growth.

Our next chapter shows just HOW we do that!

BIBLIOGRAPHY & FOOTNOTE

[1] *Beyond Discipline,* Ed Christophersen, PhD. Westport Publishers, Kansas City MO, 1990.

[2] *Emotional Intelligence,* Daniel Goleman, PhD. Bantam Books, New York, 1995.

"Emotional Savvy: Why EQ, in Addition to IQ, Is the Secret to Your Child's Success," Leslie Bennetts. Child (Magazine), Mar 1996, v11, n2, p56.

The Heart of Parenting: Raising an Emotionally Intelligent Child, John Gottman, PhD. Simon & Schuster, New York, (scheduled for Jan 1997).

[3] For a fuller discussion of the word "use", refer to Enhancement F, *Key Words.*

[4] *The Family Matters,* Public Service Campaign '95. Interview with Katie McGucken, aired July 1995. Bonneville Broadcasting Corporation. Kansas City MO.

Chapter 4

The

Yellow

Brick

Road

4

Chapter Four

The Yellow Brick Road
(Procedures to get the most out of the Think Space)

When Dorothy, in the fabled *Wizard of Oz*,[1] was trying to find the Emerald City, she fortuitously ran across a good witch who knew the way.

"Just follow the yellow brick road," the good witch motioned with her arm, "and you will get there before you know it!"

And, sure enough, just by doing as she was shown, Dorothy soon found the land of her search.

We would like to do the same for you. To help you discover how to effectively use the Think Space, let us take you down "the yellow brick road."

As parents and professional child-care providers, we are increasingly on the look-out for effective, orderly methods to manage our homes and classrooms without stifling the natural creativity of the children under our care or creating a potentially

---

abusive situation. In the first three chapters, we chronicled the development and formalization of an approach which has turned out to be one of the best tools for low-stress behavior management that we have ever found. Chapter 4 now brings you the procedural "how to's" of this wonderful tool.

After several years of trial and error, mixed with enough success "to write home about," we present the procedures that have resulted in enduring results for us. And, while every care giver will color these procedures with his or her own personality, we strongly urge you to begin with these proven steps. Then, *after* mastering what we have outlined here and after experiencing success with these procedures, we encourage you to experiment in search of improvements that are more natural and more productive for you.

Think of the Think Space as a software package for your computer or the remote control for your VCR. They both have wonderful potential, but the only way to tap their potential is to follow a very specific sequence — every time.

We suggest that, as you begin, you apply that same idea to the Think Space technique. Again, the first three chapters walked you through an introduction to this approach. But the technique doesn't work itself. Now, Chapter 4 shows you HOW to successfully apply the Think Space. How well it *works* depends on how well you *work* it, and how well you *work* it depends on how closely you *follow* these tested and proven principles.

The steps divide into three categories:

    A) BEFORE the Think Space (separation),

    B) DURING the Think Space (diffusion),

    C) AFTER the Think Space (resolution).

Now, let's walk through the steps in just that order.

A. <u>BEFORE</u> THE THINK SPACE
PREPARATIONS FOR USING THE THINK SPACE

— The "separation" phase —

1. **Prepare the space.**

    a. Choose **a carpeted spot** where the child will not be hurt if he throws himself on the floor or falls down while he carries on.

    b. Allow **about 9 sq. feet** of clear space (3' x 3'), i.e., no furniture in the space and no sharp objects nearby.

    c. Choose **a spot that can be seen** from areas where the care provider or parent will be located, i.e., just off the classroom in preschool or day care settings, or just off the family room/kitchen area in home environments. Position the child to see what is going on so that he will be motivated to return to the action he has just left.

    d. Choose an area where crying or other noises from the child will be **a minimal concern**.

    e. Make every effort to **use the same space** every time; or, if you have spaces selected in other parts of the house, still be consistent in using the exact same spot as the need arises whenever both child and provider are in that same vicinity.

Now that you have designated or prepared an appropriate place, you need to learn *how* to use the space.

2. Prepare yourself.

    a. **Commit** yourself to using the Think Space exclusively as a tool of correction, never for punishment. In fact, if you allow yourself to use this technique as a punishment (as in, *"Tommy, go to the Think Space till you can straighten out!"*), you will damage its effectiveness as a tool of correction in the future! Here's the difference: punishment looks back at the wrong done while correction looks ahead to better choices in the future. Or, you can test yourself against this "rule of thumb": the punisher sends while the corrector takes the child to the Think Space.

    b. **Believe** in the Think Space. The effectiveness of this technique is profoundly affected by your faith in this approach. Conversely, if you doubt that this approach is going to make much difference, it probably won't! You may find some situations where this approach doesn't bring the desired results, but we have found that, when administered correctly, it works with nearly total success for children between 18 months and kindergarten age.

    c. **Determine** to practice this system until it becomes natural to you. Regard it as one of the most important learning tasks of your parenting or child-care career. Why? Because most of us are so accustomed to negative behavior control, it is a sizable task just to learn to use positive methods of behavior management. Admit it. Changing negative habits to positive comes slowly and painfully. Additionally, most of us need a lot of reminders and support as we learn a different approach to children in particular, and to life in general.

d. **Read and re-read** this book, especially this chapter, Worked properly, this system will make a huge difference in how life works in the future for both you and the child or children under your care. Discuss these ideas with your parenting partner and/or your child care colleagues. Ask for constructive criticism as others see or hear you use your new technique. Treat learning this system as you would treat learning to play a musical instrument. Remember that you are developing a new skill and that "practice makes perfect." So, keep practicing until this approach becomes second nature to you. Once that happens, you will absolutely love the results!

3. Prepare the child.

a. **Be decisive.** When you decide that a child needs to spend some time in the Think Space, act on that decision immediately. However, never use anger or roughness, because you have a tool at your disposal — the Think Space — that will help the child adjust his behavior in a much more effective way than any amount of anger or words can accomplish!

b. **Offer friendly warnings sparingly.** A threat is never appropriate. Here's the difference. A friendly warning would be,

"Megan, do you need to go to the Think Space to change your attitude?"

A threat would say,

"Megan, if you don't stop that screaming, you're going to go to the Think Space!"

c. **Take — never send** — the child to the Think Space. The point is this: it is impossible to help the child with his thinking if you just send him. We ask that you absolutely understand that sending is NOT an option! If you are unable to take the child at that moment, have him stay with you until you can take him, or do something else creative. If the child resists, try the following:

If the child says, *"I don't WANT to go to the Think Space,"* you say, *"Oh, that's okay. You don't need to WANT to go there. I just need you to cooperate with me right now."*

You'll be surprised at how much resistance that one line dissolves!

If the child pulls back or falls down, just quietly and unemotionally pick the child up in your arms and carry him there. The amazing thing is that, in so doing, you are quietly demonstrating your leadership, rather than letting the child monopolize your attention while you correct him over something that has gone wrong.

If a child refuses to stay in the Think Space, refer to Enhancement D, *The Child Who "Won't" Stay in the Think Space.*

B. <u>DURING</u> THE THINK SPACE

WHAT TO DO WHILE THE CHILD IS IN THE THINK SPACE

— The "diffusion" phase —

1. Have the child stand, **touching nothing** at all. You want to avoid making this a comfortable situation. An exception is the temper tantrum, which normally includes lying down while kicking and crying. Even in that case, have the child stand as soon as he begins to quiet down.

2. Tell the child that he may continue that behavior in the Think Space and when he is **finished** you will talk; or, when he is ready to cooperate, he may come back.

   Of course, your "tongue is in your cheek," for you know that the main purpose for most every inappropriate behavior is to influence another person. When that factor is missing, the "adventure" of misbehavior is also missing. So, guess what — the behavior is simply abandoned, usually without ceremony or stress!

3. If the child is crying or fussing in any way, absolutely limit yourself to **one sentence** and one sentence only. That sentence is this:

   "When you are finished crying (or fussing), we can talk."

   The point is this: NEVER TRY TO REASON WITH A CHILD WHILE HE OR SHE IS CRYING OR FUSSING.

   Why? Because the child can't hear reason at that point. Furthermore, trying to talk through crying or fussing will undermine your ability to communicate later with that child.

----

4. Since this process needs to involve thinking, and since the child has already demonstrated inadequate thinking, it is important to **help the child redirect his thoughts.**

First, be sure the child is "finished" with any noisy behavior before you begin this step.

Then, ask the child what he is going to be thinking about. His answer will probably be, *"...not hitting Jeffrey,"* or some similar "not" (negative) thought. Here is your teachable moment.

You respond with,

"Excuse me, Andrew. Shouldn't you be thinking about correct behavior instead of incorrect behavior?"

"Yeah, I guess so," he'll say.

"Then, you need to be thinking about using your hands for helping Jeffrey, not for hurting him, okay?"

"Okay."

"Now, what are you going to be thinking about?"

"Using my hands for helping Jeffrey."

"Good, Andrew. Now, I want you to think about that for a while, and when you're ready to use your hands for helping instead of hurting, you may return to your friends."

Guess what. Nine times out of ten there will be a substantial difference in Andrew's behavior when he returns to his friends. And ten times out of ten you have taken a positive route that, at the very least, lays the foundation of great positive benefit!

Supporting this kind of positive approach, Angela Ebron, a contributor to *Family Circle*, advises, *"Tell your kids what you DO want, not what you DON'T want."* [2]

Adele Faber, co-author of *How to Be the Parent You Always Wanted to Be*, explains, "The problem with negative commands and negative reflection is that kids often just pick up the tail end of what you've said. If you say, *'Don't jump,'* they hear *'jump.'* Rephrase your sentences to emphasize the appropriate behavior: *'The sofa is for sitting'.*" [3] (sic)

In fact, some very exciting research on this subject confirms that the *real* reason a child just picks up the last part of a negative command is that the sub-conscious mind doesn't even have the ability to discern negative from positive! And since it only recognizes positive parts of communication, it hears "jump" while it completely ignores "don't"!

That's why it is so important for a child to think about positive actions rather than his negative behavior while he is in the Think Space.

5. Now, walk away and **strictly avoid any conversation or comments** (except those in point 4 above). The less attention you allow the child at this point, the better this process works. Here is where you may need to exercise extraordinary faith and self-discipline:

   • *FAITH* because, when you first try this process, you will not have the experience of seeing that a child on a sub-conscious level actually *appreciates* the opportunity to drain his emotions, to think, to center, or to settle down. Only rarely will a child leave the Think Space before quieting down. It is amazing even to us to see children as young as 18 months — children who can barely talk — totally cooperate with the procedure. (For those children who resist cooperating, refer to Enhancement D, *The Child Who "Won't" Stay in the Think Space.*)

- **SELF-DISCIPLINE** because you will either be tempted to further address the difficulty being treated (as in the "editorial monologue") or you will want to keep looking at the child to see how he is reacting to the Think Space. Of course, you have a responsibility for the safety of the child, so let your observations be coy and quick.

Remember, the success of this technique is based on the child's behavior failing to influence other people, including you. Therefore, any attention you give the child, once he is in the Think Space, actually compromises the effectiveness of the Think Space because the child's psyche will interpret your attention as success for himself!

From personal experience, we can assure you that this method is infinitely better than traditional alternatives — scolding, shouting and spanking — we have used through the years. We only wish that we had discovered earlier what we now use every day. But, so much the better for you, for you now have a tool that can make a world of difference both in the way *your kids* turn out and the way *you* turn out at the end of your day with children!

C. <u>AFTER</u> THE THINK SPACE

WHAT TO DO WHEN THE CHILD IS READY TO LEAVE THE THINK SPACE

— The "resolution" phase —

One of the main factors that makes the Think Space successful is the child's being given some personal control over his re-entry into his former environment. At a very deep level, the child appreciates this kind of trust and usually honors it in a surprisingly sincere way. Even an 18-month-old toddler who can barely talk appreciates the opportunity to drain his emotions without being stifled by a well-meaning but over-controlling care giver.

As we have mentioned in Step 2 of the previous section, the child's re-entry into his former environment falls into two options: talking with the adult care giver who has put him in the Think Space, or returning on his own without any further conversation.

1. RETURNING AFTER TALKING WITH THE ADULT SUPERVISOR

When some kind of repair work, whether physical or psychological, needs to be carried out before the child resumes his previous activity, you should have left him with something like, *"When you are ready to (talk, apologize, cooperate), I want you to tell me."*

This can be a true "teachable moment" for the child. First, because he has had time to settle down to a point where he is more open to learning. Secondly, because he quietly respects you for your restraint in not lecturing him or forcing him to do something that he was not ready to do with a sincere attitude before or during his time in the Think Space.

The Think Space

The additional benefit of delaying your talk with your child or student is that *you* have had some time to settle yourself and to think about your approach to your child or student.

Here are some approaches that we have found to work very well:

a. When your child has **offended** another child or adult (hurt, insulted, harmed a project, etc.), ask him,

> *"How can you help Kevin feel better?"*

Usual responses include "apologize," "say sorry," "help fix his work," "hug him." Normally, the child will mention only one thing. If you want him to do more, just say, "And what else?" until you get the response you are seeking or until the child has exhausted the options. At that point you still have another viable option which is to direct the offender to ask the offended child what will help.

One day, after an incident between two children, it occurred to me that the offending child (who happened to be picking on a younger new child) simply did not respect his new "friend." In fact, as I thought about it, I realized that they simply did not know each other very well.

So, after he had finished his time in the Think Space, I said,

> *"Trent, you need to get acquainted with Kevin. I would like you to help Kevin with whatever he is doing from now until lunch time (about half an hour). You let him be the leader and you be his helper. I'll be watching to see how things are going."*

And you know what happened? You guessed right. They worked together nicely without a single problem.

Furthermore, to my knowledge, they never again had another problem of that kind with each other!

Granted, not all situations will be handled that easily or that permanently, but it is safe to say that solutions which make a lasting impact are out there. We need only to be open to fresh variations in dealing with situations as they appear.

b. When the child needs a general **correction** about an attitude or particular habit, either kneel down to his level or place the child on a surface so that you are able to look him straight in the eye. Now you say,

> *"Trent, we need to talk."*

Then you should continue with questions that lead to whatever point you are wanting to make. In that way, the child is being asked to interact with you, a technique infinitely better than his listening to you lecture. To lecture is to lose, so save your energy for something that will make a difference!

c. **The Three-Choice Quiz**

When a child is ready to resume the activity which you have interrupted in favor of giving him time in the Think Space, give him the three-choice quiz. It goes like this:

> *"Trent, when you have a problem with someone else, you have three choices."*

Hold up the last three fingers of either hand, including the small finger. Now say,

1. *"You can choose to **fuss"** (point to the small finger),
2. *"You can choose to **ignore** the problem"* (point to the next finger),
3. *"Or, you can choose to **work it out"*** (point to the center finger).

Then you ask,

"Which behavior did you use . . .

the smallest behavior (point to the small finger),

or the biggest behavior" (point to the center finger)?

Of course, the answer is *the smallest behavior*, which also illustrates the relative stature of his choice!

Now you say,

"If that same problem happens again, which behavior would be a better choice?"

Your child will point to either the "ignoring" finger or to the "work it out" finger.

Then you ask the child,

"Which behavior is that?"

He will respond with either "work it out" or "ignore." You may need to help him with the names of the fingers. Be sure to affirm his excellent choice and assure him that you will be looking for that choice next time.

2. RETURNING ON HIS OWN

Since this feature of the Think Space gives some or all the control of the child's return *to the child himself*, some adults feel apprehensive, if only because this approach is so unusual. You may ask, "Where is the discipline when you use this option?"

Our experience is that children in the 18-month to five-year-old range actually appreciate the Think Space for three big reasons:

- They appreciate someone helping them to break whatever behavior it is that has captured them. The truth is that they don't like what's happening any more than you do!

- They actually appreciate — maybe even enjoy — the opportunity to show that they are developing some personal self-control, especially right after they have demonstrated the lack of it!

- The nature of the child looks for and thrives on limits, which the Think Space inherently communicates, regardless of the child's outward response.

The discipline of this option is found in the child's opportunity to exercise inner control (self-control) — actually, an opportunity to develop self-discipline. Believe it or not, we have to help our younger children come *out* of the Think Space more frequently than we have to help them stay *in* the Think Space! Here's the point: if we want our children to learn to take responsibility for their choices, we need to set up situations that encourage and effectively monitor self-discipline. Built into the Think Space option is a wonderful opportunity for children to develop the inner discipline we say we want them to develop. (Regrettably, we adults typically do precious little to encourage our children's inner controls by almost constantly telling them what to do, when to do it and where to do it!)

Now, let's continue with this option.

If you have set up the child's return to his former environment at his discretion (as in, *"When you're ready to work quietly, you may come back."*), make every effort to honor his choice, regardless of how *much* or, more realistically for an older child, how *little* time he spent in the Think Space.

The Think Space

If you tamper with that choice, you lose credibility with the child. On a sub-conscious, if not conscious, level he realizes that you don't really mean what you say, which inevitably affects his faith in other things you say.

Furthermore, when you break your commitment to the child, you actually give him the idea that he shouldn't trust his *own* judgment, which is just opposite what we want to teach. Rather, we want to help the child use the Think Space as a safe place to stay while he deals with his internal conflicts. Even if we feel the child is leaving the space too early, the best choice may just be to let him re-enter his former environment too soon, if only to point out later (perhaps, during his next time in the Think Space) that he must not have taken enough time to think about correct behavior, so he probably needs to take a few extra minutes this time.

Does that kind of thing actually happen? Yes, it surely does. Just the other day I called Andrew out of the classroom when I happened to see him trying to solve a problem with Austin by hitting him. Sheepishly, Andrew came to me without objection. I asked him about the problem and then asked if he needed some time to think about the situation. Yes, he did. So, he took a minute or so to think.

As he moved toward the classroom door, I interrupted him.

"Are you finished thinking already, Andrew?"

"Uh huh," he responded tentatively.

"So, what did you think about?"

"Not hitting."

"Oh, Andrew," I moaned quietly. *"I was hoping you would think about using your hands for helping instead of hurting!"*

"Oh yeah," he recalled quickly. *"I thought just a little. Maybe I better think longer about that too!"*

And he did!

Soon Andrew truly was ready to return to his friends (or whatever the activity was from which he was taken to spend time in the Think Space).

3. LOTS OF HUGS AND TLC

Finally, before you let the child go, spend a few moments reassuring him of your continuing love and care. Since the Think Space is largely about technique, it is all too easy to be technically correct but totally neglect the human elements of warmth and tender loving care (TLC). In our school, those elements are a given. However, it would be possible for someone to miss the spirit of our suggestions if he were to work strictly from the instructions given here.

Therefore, we need to state as strongly as possible that not one of these ideas is worth the proverbial "plugged nickel" if it is not applied with a loving and caring attitude. What is true for adults also holds for children :

**"People don't care how much you know
until they know how much you care!"**[4]

Frequently, at the close of time in the Think Space, I sit down or kneel beside the child, draw him to me and indulge in a great big mutual hug with the reassuring words, "I love you."

To operate the Think Space without this kind of commitment to nurturing the spirit of that child would render this whole approach as sterile as a neutered tom cat. You can be sure that very little positive results will come out of even the most deliberate and proper execution of the Think Space if it is not executed with lots of hugs and TLC!

So, there you have it. You have come with us up the yellow brick road right to the gates of your own "Emerald City," the Think Space. But before you enter, let's take a few moments to distinguish this unique place from the very popular (but often misused) disciplinary technique, Time-Out!

BIBLIOGRAPHY

[1] *Wonderful Wizard of Oz,* L. Frank Baum. Baronet Books/ Playmore, New York, 1989.

[2] *"Words That Work,"* Angela Ebron. Family Circle, Feb. 2, 1993, v106, n2, p7(1).

[3] *How to Be the Parent You Always Wanted to Be,* Adele Faber & Elaine Mazlish. Hypeion Publishers; International Center for Creative Thinking, 1992.

[4] *Develop the Leader Within You,* John C. Maxwell. Thomas Nelson Publishers. Nashville, TN, 1993. p117.

Chapter 5

What About Time-Out?

5

What About Time-Out?
(A comparison of Time-Out with the Think Space)

Even though the sports term "Time-Out" was first applied as a behavioral term to autistic children,[1] one thing is certain: Time-Out as a disciplinary technique for "normal" children is about as common today as spanking was common at the turn of the century!

In the CBS television documentary, *48-Hours,* titled *"Discipline; When Is It Too Much?",* [2] Dr. Ed Christophersen shows a young family how to effectively use Time-Out with a belligerent two-year-old. Happily, it worked well for the family which was using it for the TV test, which makes the point that Time-Out, when correctly applied, can be an effective behavior management resource.

The popularity of Time-Out as a discipline technique has been largely fueled during the last decade or so by the increasing resistance of parents and child rights advocates to any form of discipline or punishment that includes strong physical contact with the child.

While Time-Out, applied properly, is a fine tool to help a child learn "self-quieting skills",[2] Time-Out is frequently misused as an instrument of punishment rather than as a tool of correction. And while Time-Out as a technique generally satisfies physical non-abuse criteria, when misapplied, it can be psychologically abusive and can even reinforce the undesirable behavior it is meant to defeat![3]

"WHAT WORKS BETTER THAN TIME-OUT?"

Recently, while talking with my mother's nurse, I mentioned that we work with preschoolers. Immediately she quizzed me about her own two-year-old daughter. *"What works better than Time-Out?"* she asked expectantly.

That sort of question is common when people learn that we work with preschoolers. It seems that many parents and providers are desperately reaching out for behavior management options that are more effective than Time-Out!

The general sense is that Time-Out doesn't work as well as it once did. Perhaps its popularity has resulted in frequent misuse. Maybe, however, it's time to look at Time-Out as a disciplinary device and ask the one question that truly fuels improvement, "How can Time-Out be improved?" or even, "Is there a better way?"

To that question, we happily shout, "Eureka - we've found it!" Not that we have found a one-size-fits-all solution to behavior management of young children. Rather, we prefer to offer the Think Space as an additional option in the tool chest of child management resources. Happily, the weaknesses inherent in Time-Out are substantially addressed by the Think Space.

There are significant differences between Time-Out and the Think Space. The next page lists seven comparisons for your consideration.

Before we consider those comparisons, we want to point out that what we offer in this book shares a common foundation with Time-Out. That foundation is:

temporarily removing a child from the environment in which he is expressing inappropriate behavior.

IMPRESSIVE RESEARCH!

Research has confirmed that the above action gives a child the opportunity to refocus, which can lead to positively-altered behavior.

It would be both disrespectful and short-sighted to disassociate the Think Space from Time-Out. A review of the scientific research recorded on the Time-Out theme is impressive. Between 1964 and 1995 well over 100 separate research and study projects have detailed the results of testing nearly every imaginable aspect of the Time-Out concept when applied to both humans and animals. The general outcome of this research shows undeniably improved performance by the subjects on whom Time-Out was applied when compared with the use of other motivational techniques.

It is this body of research, then, that provides the scientific foundation on which the Think Space is built. We will be forever grateful for the dedicated efforts of hundreds of researchers who have provided a solid rationale for the use of the Time-Out principle as a valid technique for behavior modification. The bibliography at the end of this chapter lists some of the books coming out of that research detailing the effective application of Time-Out.[4]

There is a caution, however, in thinking of the Think Space as an "improved model" of Time-Out. For most people, a fresh start will be best. Here's why. If a person is accustomed to misusing Time-Out, chances are very strong that he or she will slip into the same errant habits in applying the Think Space.

Conversely, if the Think Space is presented as a fresh, new method of positive behavior management, there is a much better chance that the care giver who was misusing Time-Out will give a fresh effort to the Think Space.

To help you see the contrast between the two systems, we have created two columns for comparison:

TIME-OUT	THINK SPACE
1. The child is usually *sent* to Time-Out.	1. The child is *taken* to the Think Space.
2. Inappropriate behavior is *punished* and *repressed.*	2. Inappropriate behavior is *"finished"* without *repression.*
3. Typically Time-Out looks *backward* at wrongs done in the *past.*	3. The Think Space looks *forward* to better choices in the *future.*
4. The child's *thinking* during Time-Out is usually not *guided.*	4. The child is *guided* to *think* about *how* to respond the next time.
5. The *requirement* for exit is the completion of a pre-set amount of *time.*	5. The primary *requirement* for exit is a change of *attitude,* demonstrated by willing "cooperation.*"*
6. The amount of *time* spent is determined by an *adult.*	6. The amount of *time* spent is determined by the *child* with the help of an adult.
7. *Reconciliation* with others is not a prescribed part of Time-Out procedure.	7. *Reconciliation* with others *follows* the child's exit and is supported by an adult.

As you see, there are substantial differences between these two behavior management approaches.

Whatever the differences, however, the most important change is found in the assignment of *responsibility*. While the *responsibility* for administering Time-Out is totally in the hands of the supervising adult, *responsibility* for administering the Think Space is shared between the child and the supervising adult.

Why is this difference so important? Everyone wants to raise children who grow up to be responsible adults. However, for a myriad of reasons (which are more often excuses than they are reasons), we adults make many decisions for our children which they could help to make. Consequently, we miss many opportunities to promote a sense of responsibility and other similar character qualities such as accountability, self-control, personal discipline, independence and creative problem solving.

THE KEY IS THE USER...

Finally, whatever strengths or weaknesses may lie within either of these approaches to behavior management, the most important part is not the *method* but the *person* using the method. If a parent or care giver has a "punishment" mentality, he will likely convey his disposition using either method. Conversely, if a person is typically a positive person who centers on correction rather than punishment, he will adapt either method to carry his corrective message to the children under his care.

However, the odds for proper usage are clearly in favor of the Think Space, partly because of the detailed guidance given in this book and partly due to its basic positive, corrective structure. By reading and integrating this book into your life, you are wisely equipping yourself to maximize the potential of the Think Space while minimizing its misuse.

BIBLIOGRAPHY

[1] *"Applications of Operant Conditioning Procedures to the Behavioral Problems of an Autistic Child,"* Journal of Behavioral Psychology, Montrose Wolf, Todd Risley and Hayden Mees. Pergaman Press, 1964, v1, p305-312.

[2] *"Discipline: When Is It Too Much?"* 48 Hours News Magazine, CBS Television, first aired January, 1995.

[3] *"When Does Time-Out Become Seclusion, and What Must Be Done When This Line Is Crossed?"* Richard J. Landau and Roderick MacLeish. Residential Treatment for Children and Youth, Fine & Ambrogne, Boston MA, 1988, v6 (2), p33-38.

[4] *The Time-Out Solution,* Lynn Clark. Contemporary Books, Chicago, 1989.

Time-Out For Toddlers, James Varni & Donna Corwin. Berkley Books, New York, 1991.

"Smart Ways to Use Time-Out," Jill Hamilton. Parents' Magazine, Dec 93, v68, n12, p110 (3).

Chapter 6

WHY

the

Think

Space

Works

Chapter Six

WHY the Think Space Works
(Technical stuff behind the "magic")

Although the Think Space, when administered properly, works almost as if by "magic," there are solid, identifiable reasons *why* it works so well. If you're the type of person who likes to know what's behind the scenes of a great event or what went into the childhood of a famous person, then you will enjoy this chapter. (Even if you don't particularly care about "backstage stuff," you will still do yourself a favor to study this chapter because the better you understand this system, the better you will be able to apply it.) In any case, in this segment, we go "backstage" to meet the actors — the technical elements — behind the success of this "drama".

AN "INSIDE OUT" PHILOSOPHY

The Think Space is born out of a philosophy of child management much larger than itself. Looking at the big picture, there are two basic camps regarding the way people work with children:

- The *direct* camp, the "outside-in" philosophy, sees the *adult* as the dispenser of knowledge and wisdom and, therefore, the center of the learning process.
- The *indirect* camp, the "inside-out" philosophy, sees the *child* as the center of the learning process and the adult as facilitator.

The Think Space is a product of the second camp. It is based on a practical educational approach developed by Maria Montessori, the first female medical doctor of Italy. Working among children of the ghetto in the early 1900's, she pioneered an approach for preschool age children which now bears her name world wide. According to observers, it is "a method of educating young children that stresses the development of a child's own initiative and natural abilities . . . ." [1]

Her research, which was eventually developed into a unique, formalized approach to children under the moniker, "The Montessori Method," found that even young children (ages three through six) possess an inner teacher which is far superior to any human who touches his or her life. As she saw it, that inner teacher can and will guide the child to what needs to be learned when the child is ready in a far more sensitive way than external teachers can determine for that child. In her book, *The Absorbent Mind,* she writes:

> *"There is . . . in every child a painstaking teacher, so skillful that he obtains identical results in all children in all parts of the world. The only language men ever speak perfectly is the one they learn in babyhood, when no one can teach them anything!"* [2]

Then she highlights her thoughts with this provocative insight:

> *"We teachers can only help the work going on, as servants wait upon a master."* [2]

In her day, this idea was so novel that she became a frequent recipient of extreme responses, from persecution to adulation. But she was a confident and intelligent person who, through perseverance and subsequent success with even the least likely of children, made her mark on her world. Thankfully, she documented her work in several writings including *The Montessori Method* [3] and *The Absorbent Mind.* [2] Through the years that followed, those two works provided the foundation of an influence that has found its way into the thinking of educators and child psychologists around the globe.

While the outside-in approach is quicker and more natural for untrained adults, that kind of direct tactic actually dulls rather than develops the natural sensitivities of a child. In the end you make him more and more dependent on external guidance rather than develop his superior internal guidance instincts.

AS YOUNG PARENTS . . .

As young parents, we relied almost entirely on the outside-in approach. While we knew that other approaches were out there, we were guilty of "throwing out the baby with the bath water," for we lumped all non-direct child management methods into the "permissive" camp, which we feared would inevitably lead to a lack of discipline in our children. We were sure we did not want an undisciplined result, so we built our operating philosophy on the direct outside-in approach.

It was only after we were exposed to the Montessori Method and had years of experience applying her approach to children that we began to experiment with the Think Space, which turns out to be a direct descendent of Montessori's thinking. While its association with Montessori is neither formal nor intentional, the

The Think Space

Think Space uses the same beginning points as the Montessori Method and, as such, is a natural consequence of integrating her indirect approach into child management.

In a word, then, the Think Space is a practical application of the Montessori philosophy which aims at developing the child from the *inside out* rather than from the *outside in!*

With that background behind us, let's move on to the other players in our drama called the Think Space.

The Think Space works because

IT IS BASED ON A GROUP OF

ASSUMPTIONS

THAT, EXPERIENCE SHOWS, ARE ALMOST ALWAYS TRUE AND ACCURATE.

Some of the assumptions:

1. A child spending time in the Think Space is motivated toward inner change by his desire to return to the environment from which he has been removed.

2. A child learns right from wrong quickly at a very early age (provided his care givers have helped him find those markers from early on).

3. A child's "inner teacher"[3] will help him integrate appropriate behavior into his life even more efficiently than he will learn those same lessons through external "lectures" and other forms of adult domination.

4. The Think Space encourages a child to be accountable to his "inner teacher," which moves him toward personal, independent behavior management (called self-control in adults).

5. A child wants to do right, if only for the approval of his parents or providers.

6. By spending time in the Think Space, a child will move from a basically emotional state of mind to a more rational frame of mind.

7. By being moved away from the scene of conflict, a child will gain a larger and less selfish perspective.

8. A child appreciates time to settle down.

9. A child likes peace and harmony in his world more than conflict and discord.

10. A child will discontinue anti-social behavior when it fails to reward him.

You may question any or all of these assumptions and that is okay. However, experience has taught us that these assumptions are almost always accurate, and that any disagreement on their accuracy is usually more a problem of semantics than actual disagreement with the spirit of the assumption.

The balance of this chapter, while not strictly organized according to the above assumptions, is actually an expansion of them under other headings.

Moving on, then, to that expansion, this approach to behavior management works because

IT BEGINS BY RECOGNIZING THE CHILD AS

THE ULTIMATE PRAGMATIST.

The preschool child is the ultimate pragmatist. He only repeats behavior that has worked at least once! The flip side of that coin is this: behavior which is intended to collect attention, if unrewarded, will *eventually* be abandoned and replaced with new experiments until the child finds something that *does* work.

In a nutshell, the "magic" of the Think Space is found in providing an orderly way to diffuse and thereby disempower inappropriate behavior.

Most of us grew up under, and as adults have operated by, the exact opposite notion — that the best way to stop unwanted behavior was to confront it — scold it, spank it, punish it in some way. The unstated belief is, "The more attention you give a misbehavior, the more convinced the child will be that he should discontinue that activity."

But think back. How well did that approach work on you as a child? And, how well has it worked for you as a parent or provider? Did it really work well enough for you to continue that same practice?

Whether you answer, "Yes," or "No," please pause to consider two ideas, *validation* and *control.*

The Think Space works because

IT GIVES A CREATIVE ALTERNATIVE TO

THE VALIDATION ISSUE.

Every moment you spend personally and verbally confronting or, in any way, addressing a misbehavior with traditional methods, you *validate* that behavior as an instrument of power. While you are intending to defeat the misbehavior, you are actually admitting its power. The point is that punishments which focus on the wrong someone has done, inadvertently *reinforce* the very behavior they were intended to stop. In addressing the behavior, you usually end up *empowering* it rather than *defeating* it!

Why do criminals so often return to the very crimes for which they spend years in prison? Indeed, why do children frequently follow precisely the same pattern? Though the reasons are complex, at least one clue to the mystery lies in this fact: while enduring their punishments, those being punished are constantly reminded of the power of their misbehavior. The power-thirsty disposition, in turn, can hardly wait until it has an opportunity to express that power again, even if it leads to the same end!

Doesn't the general failure of correction by punishment urge us to seek out a more effective system, especially for our children? Happily, the Think Space provides that opportunity.

Next, let's move to a topic that is generally misunderstood and, consequently, mishandled by almost every adult who works with children.

The Think Space works because

IT RECOGNIZES THE POWER TO

CONTROL

AS A PRIMARY DRIVER OF THE CHILD'S PSYCHE.

While children dearly desire the approval of their parent or supervising adult, the fact *is* that children *do* "disobey" their parent or care provider, both consciously and unconsciously. Why would a child risk doing something that he *knows* will not meet with the approval of his parent or care provider? We suggest that most inappropriate behavior comes out of an even higher priority than gaining approval.

Have you noticed that much, if not most, of the conflicts between children and adults or even between children themselves is about *power*? Human nature loves power, whether direct or indirect. Watch the TV and video scenarios that children re-enact in their play. Do not most of them deal in some way with the wielding of power? In recent years we have seen dozens of would-be Teenage Mutant Ninja Turtles, then Batman, followed closely by a rainbow of (would you believe?) Power Rangers. And what is the theme? POWER! But not just power for the sake of power. It's the power to *control;* the ability to *control* people and circumstances under the influence of that power.

So comes the question, "How can we tap into a child's desire for power and control and still maintain an appropriate leadership role as the adult supervisor of the child?"

Chapter 6: WHY The Think Space Works

The Think Space is a part of the answer, since

IT DEALS WITH THE CHILD'S NATURAL DESIRE TO HAVE SOME

CONTROL

OVER HIS OWN WORLD.

Since most children, at a very early age, find out that direct control doesn't work very well on people bigger than themselves (i.e., their supervising adults), they get very good at *indirect control*.

So what is *INDIRECT CONTROL?*

Almost everything that goes wrong between adults and children is, on some level, about control; begging mommie for another story after she says she has already read the last story; putting up such a fuss at the grocery store that Bobbie gets some treat just to appease him; arguing about which clothes to wear.

SURPRISE! MICKEY'S IN CHARGE!

Recently, a close friend and the mother of an exceptionally active and precocious four-year-old was telling me about her frustrations with her son's trying antics at home — doing things on purpose that he knows are wrong, then repeating the exact same things for which he has just been punished! The list went on and on.

"He isn't like that at preschool," she added. *"Just at home."*

I began to be suspicious. Then she voiced her most revealing remark.

"He's not manipulative," she quipped, *"just blatant and bold!"*

The Think Space

STOP!

Did you hear what she said: *"The child isn't manipulative"?*
I smiled.

"My dear," I carefully quizzed my friend, *"did you realize that Mickey is in control, whether or not you think he is manipulative?"*

"Really?" she asked in disbelief.

I just grinned.

What a classic illustration of the way most adults misunderstand control! As long as the parent or care provider is addressing the child, whether for positive or negative reasons, the parent is surrendering control to the child, at least for the moment. And, while that kind of control is not necessarily all wrong in the short term, the unsuspecting parent or care provider needs to realize what is going on.

What do you think might change now that my friend is beginning to see that Mickey is, after all, manipulating her? He may be doing it in a way that is more outright than devious, but, nevertheless, is luring her into his web of control!

That, in fact, was her next question.

"Okay then, wise guy," she retorted good-naturedly. *"What can I do to change the situation?"*

INDIRECT CONTROL . . . SO SUBTLE

Indirect control, used every day by preschool children of all ages, is so subtle that it usually goes unnoticed. In the end, the unsuspecting adult sees the *results* of losing control, but doesn't know *how* that situation came to be! Even though most people,

----

including parents and providers, do not usually even recognize, much less understand, this form of control, it may be the most frequently used in child-adult relationships.

As long as an adult is addressing a child, whether that recognition is for positive or for negative reasons, the child has the adult's attention and sees himself, if only sub-consciously, in control of the supervising adult. That's why the child who is lacking in attention or who is feeling the need to control, will use, even invent, behaviors that capture the attention of his parent or care provider, even though he knows he is doing wrong and even if he knows he will "get into trouble" for his actions. The inescapable fact is that, ". . . a preschooler's most priceless possession is his parents' attention." [4]

Ironically, his sub-conscious mind knows that the very process of being "disciplined" will still give him the attention of his adult supervisor and, therefore, a few more moments of control! And, even though the child may not be *intentionally* vying for control, his supervising adult ends up innocently handing control to him, if only by default!

So, with these ideas on the table, you may be asking, "With control being such a native part of the human drive, are you daring to suggest that the child be denied any and all forms of control until he has his own children over which to wield control? And are you, indeed, advocating a system which enhances the adult's natural tendency to *control* children?"

Good questions . . . and a resounding, "OF COURSE NOT," to both!

The Think Space works so well because

IT PRESENTS A SAFE WAY TO RETURN SOME

CONTROL

TO THE CHILD.

Think about this: *"You gain control by giving control."*[5] Sounds intriguing, but what does it mean?

When you take a child to the Think Space, you have the opportunity to release two controls: the immediate stopping of an unacceptable behavior, and the re-entry of the child into the environment which he has just left.

STOPPING UNACCEPTABLE BEHAVIOR

As a busy parent, I frequently found myself imposing my own time priorities on my children. I wanted my kids to stop crying "right now," or insisted that the child quit whatever irritating behavior was bothering me "before I lose my patience, my mind, or whatever (you name it)."

While that approach works on one level, it totally short-circuits another. It's the difference between "winning the battle and losing the war." Here's what I mean.

When you attack an unwelcome behavior with the emotional resolve that you are going to stop it "right now" (and we are all guilty of doing this), you may get the job done in the short term, but you have not allowed that behavior to accomplish anything inside the child, except to further convince the child of your ability to dominate! But here is the good news. That moment of potential learning will inevitably be presented again, probably in the near future, and in an even more extreme way! You will then have another chance to do it right!

Chapter 6: WHY The Think Space Works

Next time, if you allow the Think Space to work *for* you, the child will be given the opportunity to *finish* whatever therapeutic value there is in a particular action without forcing its immediate closure. Again, since the inherent goal of most abrasive behavior is its effect on other people, when the opportunity to influence others is removed, the unacceptable behavior is usually abandoned.

Here's the point. When you as a parent or care provider give up the notion that *the sooner a particular behavior is stopped, the sooner everything will be better,* you take a huge step toward allowing a more wholesome development of the child under your care. It may not be as quick an approach, but it will pay off in the long run. It's like an investment. You have to wait for a while for the investment of your self-control to pay off, but it will have a much bigger and better payoff than you would see if you were to forcibly stop something that you find unacceptable or offensive. (The obvious exception to this policy, of course, is when the safety, whether physical or psychological, of the children under your care is *truly* being endangered.)

Understand, however, that if something needs to be addressed, it is usually best to take immediate and decisive (although gentle) action. Strictly avoid *threatening* your children with your possible action and use warnings sparingly.[6]

RETURN TO PREVIOUS ACTIVITY

The second control that you relinquish is the timing of the child's return to his previous activity. Instead of *you* deciding when the child may re-enter the classroom, the family game or play with friends, under the Think Space system, the child's re-entry is determined by the *child* more than by the *adult.*

The Think Space

Of course, how well that actually works out really depends on how well you "set up" the child's time in the Think Space. Although you have already seen the extensive explanation of recommended procedures for administering the Think Space in Chapter 4, we want to stress, again, the two basic ways to set up the child's stay in the Think Space:

1. Tell the child, *"When you are ready to (cooperate, do your own work, etc.), then you may join us,"* or

2. When some issue needs to be discussed with the child before he returns to the group or his aborted activity, you should say, *"When you are ready to talk with (whomever), let me know."*

In either case, you have given up total control in favor of a shared control.

The "bottom line" on the matter of control is this: as adults responsible for the nurturing of the children under our care, we are able to have a much more effective impact on our children when we work *with* their human nature than when we respond in *direct opposition* to it as we so often tend to do. When we begin working in harmony with human nature, we reduce much of the stress normally associated with managing children, while increasing the efficiency of our efforts to guide and nurture them.

We have found that by providing ways to help the child feel that he has some control of his life, he is infinitely easier to handle. Consequently, *your life is easier because you are walking in step with the way a child feels rather than in opposition to it!*

Next, we will show you that the Think Space works so well because

IT HELPS THE ADULT ASSIST THE CHILD IN THE

CONTROL OF ATTITUDE.

If a positive attitude is an important trait of truly successful people, as pointed out in Elwood Chapman's *Attitude: Your Most Priceless Possession,*[7] then does it not make good sense to train our young to take responsibility for their attitudes from their earliest days on earth?

The Think Space provides that opportunity, for it can also serve as the "Pout Space," the "Angry Space," the "Cry Space," etc. In other words, it is fine to use the Think Space as a sanctuary where children have the freedom to exhaust the common behavioral challenges of childhood without the fear of retaliation, being "put down" or being belittled — a place where they can literally take the time to "settle" without being pushed or badgered. The Think Space, like no other formalized behavioral management technique known to us, presents the opportunity for basic training in one of the *few* arenas over which we humans have final control, the control of our own attitudes. This opportunity is especially highlighted with the Think Space, since some form of "attitude adjustment" is always a requirement for re-entry of the child into his former environment!

And do you know what? Somehow, most children intuitively appreciate that kind of direction. Their instincts tell them that there *has* to be a better way of dealing with this or that. But most children just have not developed the tools or the personal discipline to adjust their attitudes on their own, thus the need for some external support from their adult care provider. Regardless of what your child's outer response may be, you *must* understand that, on a deeper level, your child is appreciating your help, even though his present demeanor would lead you to believe otherwise!

WHY USE "ATTITUDE"?

Before we move on, let's ask *why* we should use a complex adult word like "attitude" with children? Can children actually understand such a complicated idea?

First, children have the ability to learn words well beyond the normal vocabulary of our cultural expectations. Surely you can recall instances where you have heard a child use a word that you wouldn't think he is old enough to handle, much less understand! Now just think. If a child picks up advanced words from hearing them on a *casual basis*, how much more likely is it that a child can learn complex adult words and ideas that are *intentionally* presented to him?

Second, a child (just like any other human) learns the meanings of words from the *context* in which they are used long before he is able to articulate the meanings of those same words.

Third, a child's understanding of a word is reinforced through the *consistent use* of that same word or set of words in similar situations, such as using the word "attitude" in the context of the Think Space.

Fourth, a child's understanding of a word or idea is further defined as other words are introduced to explain the first idea. In our case, for example, while preparing to take a child to the Think Space, we frequently use the words "cooperate" and "cooperation" in the place of the word "attitude." In so doing, the child readily equates the same idea to the two expressions, "change of attitude" and "ready to cooperate."

Admittedly, the result that we want from a child spending time in the Think Space is *a change in verbal or overt behavior.* However, when we attach more general terms to those needed changes, we are able to use fewer words in correcting whatever it is that needs attention.

Fifth, a child's understanding of a word such as "attitude" is further refined when he is *promptly rewarded* for a perceived change in attitude while in the Think Space. In other words, as soon as the child indicates that he is ready to cooperate, you can say, *"Thanks for changing your attitude. Let's go."*

Another reason for the success of the Think Space is that

IT DEMONSTRATES AND APPLIES

LIMITS,

SOMETHING THAT THE CHILD BOTH WANTS AND NEEDS.

Everyone plays games. Games that are formalized endure because they have rules. The mission of the rules is to establish order and, in turn, make the game fun and fair for everyone. When rules are ignored, the players quit having fun and the game is abandoned in favor of something that is more fun — usually some *other* activity that also has rules!

We humans are funny that way. We know we need rules, but we try hard to avoid showing that we accept them. (Even the person who professes to not like rules has already adopted self-imposed rules that govern his life!) But it isn't necessarily the rules that we don't like. What we reject are rules that don't make sense to us or that somehow conflict with our personal identity.

The Think Space

Even the teenager who seems bent on ignoring the rules of his family, on a subliminal level still wants his parents to tell him when enough is enough. Frequently heard is the story of the teen in trouble with the law who accusingly turns to his father or mother with, *"I just wanted you to say 'no'!"*

The teenager who admits that he wanted his parents to say "no" was the same preschooler whose parents found it difficult to set limits in the early years or who used "no" in the wrong way.

RULES ARE LIMITS.

Believe it or not, children love rules — limits. To them rules and limits are fun. They instinctively know that their very security depends on limits, for the essence of security is just that.

By definition, security is:
1. Freedom from risk or danger; safety.
2. Freedom from doubt, anxiety, or fear; confidence.
3. Something that gives or assures safety.[1]

Are not all three of those definitions about limiting what IS and what is NOT allowed into the place of safety? Therefore, security is about limits, pure and simple!

While few adults will argue the child's need for security, somehow the setting and enforcing of limits in their own child's life is far more difficult to execute than it is to talk about! Maybe it's the effort required. Maybe the adult is afraid that he will be applying unimportant limits — limits that unnecessarily restrict at the expense of exploration and growth. Or, maybe the adult doesn't understand that limits in some areas actually encourage growth in other areas.

Chapter 6: WHY The Think Space Works

As you know, children are highly attracted to "the tube" (TV). If we would allow it, some of our students would spend all day every day in front of the TV, even though we watch no commercial TV, only approved videos. But, because we limit "tube time" to two short periods every day, the students turn their inquisitive energies to other classroom projects, thereby expanding abilities that would otherwise remain dormant or underdeveloped.

Whatever the reason for an adult's not applying limits, the truth is that those adults are often the same adults who simply lack safe and workable methods of setting boundaries. Well, here is good news!

The Think Space is a place that helps the child to understand limits — what *is* and what *is not* acceptable in the world that he and his adult care provider share. What helps a child to stay in the Think Space without immediate supervision is his instinctive sense that he needs limits. He also understands, if only on a sub-conscious level, that he needs some quiet time to process the limits that are presently confronting him.

The caution that we all need to observe, however, is to help the child know *how* to grow in acceptable areas. Therefore, with every limitation, there needs to be positive instruction that shows the child where he is allowed to grow. Of course, the child will grow in *some* direction, for that is the nature of the child. The task of both parent and provider, then, is to channel that growth *into* productive activity and *away* from destructive action.

VISUALIZATION: AN ESSENTIAL LINK TO CHANGE

Again, the Think Space, if administered properly, provides the child an opportunity to think through and to *visualize* correct responses within established limits: responding appropriately to a toy grabber (thereby being encouraged to learn to "work things out"), to keep his hands on his own work (learning focus and project completion) or to speak with his "inside voice" (learning respect and self-control).

. That visualization precedes actualization is a concept taught widely by practical psychologists and motivational speakers in recent years. In his *You'll See It When You Believe It*, Wayne Dyer points out that,

> "... *thoughts, when properly nourished and internalized, will become a reality in the world of form. You see, we think in pictures and these pictures become our own inner reality.*" [8]

Giving a child time to think about positive alternatives to his misbehavior is infinitely better than just talking to him, scolding, intimidating or spanking him. Children need time to process the events that enter their lives, just as *you* need time to process the "stuff" that enters *your* life! Life is simply too precious and too short to allow a child to repeat the same mistakes over and over without dedicating some intentional thought time as part of the correction process. Thinking helps people accept limits. Talking, by itself, simply is not enough.

And that is all we will say now about back stage — the technical elements — of the Think Space. Suffice it to say, however, human nature being as complicated as it is, other factors in each individual influence each child's response to the Think Space.

Still, while we recognize
and fully support the
uniqueness of each
individual, the reason
that this method works so
well with so many people
is this:
**THE THINK SPACE IS
BASED MORE ON THE
WAYS PEOPLE ARE
ALIKE THAN IT IS ON
THE WAYS IN WHICH
WE DIFFER!**

BIBLIOGRAPHY & FOOTNOTE

[1] *The American Heritage Dictionary of the English Language,* Third Edition is licensed from Houghton Mifflin Company. Copyright © 1992 by Houghton Mifflin Company.

[2] *The Absorbent Mind,* Maria Montessori; translated from the Italian by Claude A. Claremont.   Theosophical Publishing House, Adyar, India, 1961.

[3] *The Montessori Method,* Maria Montessori; translated from the Italian by Anne E. George. Frederick A. Stokes Company, New York, 1912.

[4] *Discipline Without Shouting or Spanking,* Jerry Wyckoff & Barbara Unell. Meadowbrook Press (dist. by Simon & Schuster), New York, 1984. p51.

[5] A paraphrazing of the primary message of the book, *Winning by Letting Go,* Elizabeth Brenner. Harcourt Brace Jovanovich Publishing Company, San Diego CA, 1987.

[6] See Enhancement H, *Threats, Warning and Counting,* for a fuller discussion on this issue.

[7] *Attitude: Your Most Priceless Possession,* Elwood Chapman. Crisp Publications, Los Altos CA, 1987.

[8] *You'll See It When You Believe It,* Wayne W. Dyer. W. Morrow Publishing Company, New York, 1989. p56.

Chapter 7

A
New
Lease
On
Life

. . .

With

Kids!

7

Chapter Seven

A New Lease On Life . . .
With Kids!
(To believe is to see!)

THE JOY OF CHILDREN

Children are to be enjoyed, not endured.

When Alex Comfort published his landmark manual, *The Joy of Sex* in 1972,[1] he borrowed an idea that had been used as early as 1964 by Irma Rombauer in The *Joy of Cooking*[2] and by Pearl Buck in *The Joy of Children.*[3] Together, they synchronously captured a notion that would birth a whole generation of literature using the "joy" concept. A brief trip through a title index at any major public library will reveal nearly 150 titles[4] that begin with *The Joy of...*, from *The Joy of Bach,* to *The Joy of Worship.* The message here — people want to enjoy what they do. Without joy, life becomes tedious, meaningless. Without joy, people lose focus. Priorities get skewed. Depression sets in. Even suicide seems a reasonable alternative in the absence of joy.

And, there is another message — in the plethora of "joy" books there is only a handful of books that relate to children *(The Joy of Parenthood, The Joy of Pregnancy, The Joy of Natural Childbirth)*. The one book specifically titled *The Joy of Children* is a pictorial digest based on the 1960 White House Conference on Children and Youth, not a manual on finding joy in working with children.

Do you find it ironic that *The Joy of Sex* (actually, the prelude to creating children) should have helped to spawn the "joy" series, but a similar book about the consequence of sex would take many years to emerge? As a matter of fact, it would be 21 years before the first book on nurturing children would be published that named "joy" in its title!

Time is not the issue; it's been 25 years since authors began following the examples of Rombauer, Buck and Comfort. Talent is not the point; hundreds of thousands of titles on almost every conceivable subject have entered the Library of Congress since *The Joy of Sex* was published, including over 600 titles on family & child development. Of course, writers of such books *do* have their own brains. Doing a take-off on *The Joy of Sex* may seem too simple, even plagiaristic. Okay, we'll give you that.

WHERE'S THE JOY?

But, where are the child management books that even infer joy in their titles? While our search could have missed something that's out there, we find only four parenting books that appeal to "joy" or name any synonym of joy in their titles!

Of course, many books both encourage and show the reader ways of making raising children a happy experience. Bill Cosby, in his delightful book, *Fatherhood,*[5] comes close to capturing the joy potential in parenting, but his book, too, is filled with accounts of child-rearing frustrations, although cleverly disguised with typical Cosby humor.

Looking at the big picture, allow us to ask a provocative question: "Could the hidden message be that raising children is such an overwhelming task and carries such ominous consequences, that the "joy" factor is nearly obscured?"

While the *tasks* and *consequences* of child management are not exactly the focus of this book, it is enough to point out that what we offer in these pages certainly can help to create <u>and</u> restore *joy* to the process of dealing with children. **We can truly say that if someone had given us the tool we have detailed between the covers of this book, our days with our own children would have been infinitely happier, with stress reduced by half — at least!**

EVERY DAY IS JUST SO EXCITING . . .

Thinking along these lines, my mind turns to a day when I was visiting my friend, Bob, and his family.

"The thing I love about kids," mused Bob as he watched his children play, *"is that every day is so fresh and exciting to them."*

Bob was my supervisor, but far from ordinary. Even though he was constantly exposed to colossal negative pressures in the work we performed (collision repair), he had mastered the discipline of maintaining a positive attitude in a business overrun with problematic circumstances. With uncommon discipline, he had learned to make his negative world positive just by controlling his personal attitude.

But even Bob, as successful as he was in personal attitude control, was always refreshed in seeing the excitement and freshness that children bring to life. Not just *his* children, although they were two of the loveliest little specimens of sparkle that one could ever hope to find, but almost *all* children share a similar view of each new day. They can hardly wait to do the next thing. Not yet victimized by life's disappointments that suck away joy like a giant vacuum cleaner, and loaded with creative, exploratory energy, they plunge into the events of every day with the total trust that today will be another "blast."

SO HERE'S THE BOTTOM LINE . . .

Wouldn't it be wonderful if we would approach parenting and child management with the joy of children? In fact, could it be that that is part of what Jesus meant when he said,

> *"Unless you become optimistically enthusiastic ('high' on joy) like little children, you cannot enter (experience the true excitement of) the kingdom of God"?*[6]

We have seen occasional examples of both parents and providers who actually seem to enjoy working with little ones day after day. Our daughter, now a college grad, is one of those. For years she has managed children with the joy and energy of a child — as if she never left childhood herself. The vast majority of us, however, are not so naturally gifted. The rest of us need to be more intentional, more disciplined about maintaining an attitude of joy in our work with children.

Obviously, joy is the product of much more than a behavioral management tool or a technique. Let us put to rest any suspicion that we suggest such a simplistic approach to joy in managing children. However, a tool can help a lot. Life is that way.

One simple, little idea or technique can be much bigger than itself, simply because everything in life is tied to everything else.

Therefore, when we find a better way to handle a task, especially a difficult one like raising children, everything else is made simpler.

Likewise, the approach we have taught in this book can give you "a new lease on life." At least, give it a chance. It works for us. It works for the parents who have children in our school, and it works for many of our friends in the child care business. It can also work for you, and, in the process, help you to experience the joy that children are intended to bring to your life.

TO BELIEVE IS TO SEE!

When Lucy, one of four children in C.S. Lewis' *The Lion, The Witch and The Wardrobe*,[7] ventured into the dark clothes closet of a spare bedroom during a game of hide and seek with her brothers and sister, she was serendipitously drawn into the marvelous world of Narnia. This new country, a totally unexpected discovery, would carry her into a time warp of adventure unlike anything she had ever experienced. Wanting to share that magical land with her siblings, she requested permission to return to her earth world to invite her brothers and sister to join her.

Skeptical of their younger sister, the older three searched through the closet, only to find just what they expected — smelly old clothes and stinky moth balls. Deciding that Lucy was just teasing them, they promptly began to ridicule her childish play.

In time, the wise old professor, in whose house they were living, learned of the tension between Lucy and her siblings.

Sitting down with the two older children, he helped them come to believe that Lucy was probably telling the truth.

Hearing this story for the first time, my mind went to a truism which I so wanted to share with Lucy's siblings as I unconsciously entered their story. I wanted to join the professor, look those kids straight in the eyes and give them some wisdom that I had gathered from my reading. *"Look, you kids,"* I would have said, *"you have to believe it to see it!"* [8]

As it turned out, that is exactly what happened: they believed and soon, through the miracle of believing, joined Lucy in a marvelous "lifetime" of experiences in the land called Narnia.

And that, my friends, is a vital key to making the Think Space work — you have to begin by believing that it will work!

THE "MISSY" ATTACK SYNDROME

Consider this ordinary example from the animal world. Why does Missy, our neighbor's feisty little poodle, go after one stranger but leave another alone? Both strangers can walk the same way, dress the same and talk the same. Yet, there is something that triggers the dog into hassling one stranger while she will hardly notice the other one.

Very simple. That trigger is nothing physical or visible. In fact, it is something that each of them carries but neither of them can touch. It's that intangible element, attitude — what each of them *believes* about the dog. The *fearful* stranger draws Missy's attacks while the *confident* stranger will be ignored. Make no mistake, the dog can sense who has confidence and who doesn't!

Children are much the same way. Because their sensitivities are still uncluttered in the preschool years, they can sense when their parents and care providers are confident and when they are fearful or tentative. And just like Missy, most children, especially those who *need* time in the Think Space, will take every opportunity to neutralize your leadership when given the opportunity!

Any time you use a behavioral management technique with a tentative attitude — an attitude that lacks confidence — the child is sure to sense your insecurity. To the child, that lack of confidence tells him one thing and one thing only. You are surrendering control to him! Guess what. In just a few moments, he will test your confidence, and if your confidence fails that test, the child simply assumes control!

IT FEEDS ON CONFIDENCE

So it is with the Think Space. Its ability to work for you depends, in large part, on the level of confidence you have in this tool. Obviously, in the outset you will have questions and apprehensions, even fears, all of which can quickly lead to the failure of the Think Space. Failure in the early stages needs to be avoided. Why? Because a lack of success could easily discourage you, pushing you to revert to your old ways, however unproductive and damaging they may be, simply because you need to survive!

That is exactly the reason for our taking the time to support this technique with both practical illustrations and technical background material. We want you to be successful from the very first time you use this powerful tool!

So, as you learn the steps and procedures that make the Think Space work, be certain to remember that the success of the Think Space depends, in large part, on the strength of your belief in its viability. "You'll *see* it when you *believe* it!"[8]

The Think Space

Now, before we leave this final chapter, we need to call attention to Enhancements A through I which follow this chapter. **They are not optional. In fact, they are "required reading"!**

The only reason they are at the end of the book instead of in the main text is to help you stay focused on the main idea being presented at that time. Here are the coming Enhancements and what they cover:

A. *Cautions* to help you avoid needless mistakes in the application of the Think Space.

B. *How to transfer the stress* of child management to the Think Space.

C. Using the Think Space with *older children.*

D. Handling *the child who resists* staying in the Think Space.

E. Using the Think Space *in public.*

F. Three key *words to help* the Think Space run properly and three *words to avoid.*

G. Using the Think Space as an alternative to *coaxing* a child.

H. Strong words about *threats, warnings and counting.*

I. Important insights on *the cry,* that all-purpose contrivance that the child uses for everything from survival to mutiny!

We anticipate that, as you use the Think Space, you will develop your own special ways of applying this technique to make it work best for you and your children. In fact, we fully expect some care providers to make improvements on the Think Space that we will want to use in future editions of this volume.

Please address your comments to:

THE THINK SPACE

PO Box 4490
Overland Park, KS 66204-4490

Phone (913) 341-9550
Fax (913) 341-9552

Email: crichert@dwd.com
or visit our Internet website at
http://www.dwd.com
(dwd = Discipline Without Damage)

BIBLIOGRAPHY & FOOTNOTE

[1] *The Joy of Sex,* Alex Comfort, ed. Simon & Schuster, New York, 1972.

[2] *The Joy of Cooking,* Irma von Starkloff Rombauer. Bobbs-Merill Publishers, 1964.

[3] *The Joy of Children,* Pearl S. Buck. J. Day Publishers, 1964.

[4] The Kansas City MO public library lists 148 titles that begin with the words *"The joy of . . ."*

[5] *Fatherhood,* Bill Cosby. Doubleday & Company, Garden City NY, 1986.

[6] *The Amplified New Testament (Matt. 18:3),* Ken Taylor. Moody Press, Chicago, 1962.

[7] *The Lion, the Witch and the Wardrobe,* C.S. Lewis. Macmillan Publishing Company, New York, 1992.

[8] *You'll See It When You Believe It,* Wayne W. Dyer. W. Morrow Publishing Company, New York, 1989. p56.

Enhancements

to

Help

the

Think

Space

Work

Even

Better!

Enhancement A

Cautions

about the use of the Think Space

Overuse
Underuse
Exclusions
Consistency
Positive Direction
Corrective Interaction
Child's Bedroom as Think Space

OVERUSE

When you begin to experience success with the Think Space, it will be a temptation to take a child there for every little infraction that comes along. Be sure, however, that a judicious and sparing use of the Think Space will have more meaning for the children under your care than an every-minute-of-the-day use of this facility.

Other useful techniques may include Time-Out, natural consequences [e.g., losing a privilege that has been abused], repetitious role playing, and redirected activity. Even ignoring a one-time mistake can be a useful technique under certain circumstances. Watch for our sequel to this book, *Discipline Without Damage*, in which we detail many other non-abusive approaches to behavior management which we have found to be both safe and successful.

Using our 12-student preschool as a guideline, even the most difficult day will see the Think Space occupied no more than eight to ten times (and often only two or three times), totaling no more than 25 minutes out of our 660-minute school day, a paltry four percent of the time. But, while four percent is only a small fraction of our school hours, what a wonderful difference that little fraction has made in our lives! (You may need to use the Think Space more frequently in the outset than you will use it later, i.e., until your child or children become more accustomed to the conduct you expect.)

UNDERUSE

It is quite possible to use the Think Space too little just as it is possible to overuse the practice. Familiarity with the procedure will help the child to use the Think Space for its intended outcome. For the parent or care provider, its use needs to be frequent enough to help him develop a consistent and efficient technique. As we have already pointed out, the adult who wants to make the most of this opportunity should develop his techniques just as he would practice a musical instrument. The bottom line — "practice makes perfect" (at least, a lot better).

EXCLUSIONS

While we have emphasized the potential effectiveness of this approach for a wide variety of behavioral situations, we must be careful to emphasize that it should not be regarded as the answer to all disruptive behavior for all children. Of particular concern are four conditions that predispose a child to irregular behavior which should rarely, if ever, be treated with the Think Space:

1. *Crying from fear or insecurity*

   When a child is frightened or is feeling rejected or abandoned, he needs warmth and acceptance, not separation. Placing a child who is experiencing those emotions into the Think Space is likely to be interpreted by the child as more of the same (abandonment and rejection) and will merely reinforce the child's insecurity.

2. *Crying from physical injury*

   If a child is crying due to physical injury caused by his own or someone else's error, the child needs to receive loving comfort. To send a child to the Think Space for crying when he is injured is to send the message that tough kids don't cry, or that crying is the activity of weaklings — a message that we definitely want to avoid.

3. *Irregular behavior due to chemical imbalance within the body*

   If a child is experiencing a radical imbalance of the chemicals which the body uses to function or is responding to foreign chemicals in his external environment, he may very well experience behavioral consequences that are beyond his control. In those cases, the provider needs to use extra patience. If such a condition is suspected, the parent or provider should take immediate steps to have the child evaluated professionally and actively search for a behavior management plan or environment suitable to the child's needs and abilities.

4. *Disruptive behavior from mentally and emotionally-challenged children*

Mentally and emotionally-challenged children frequently defy all our best-laid plans and procedures. They are the behavioral counterparts to the inexperienced volleyball team that is hard to defeat because its play is so unpredictable. Likewise with the mentally and emotionally-challenged, their responses to set procedures are frequently unpredictable with the outcome that what may work perfectly on one exceptional child may elicit a totally opposite response in another child with the same clinical diagnosis. Children in these categories are best handled by those trained to work with them who may or may not choose to use the Think Space.

While the above list "disqualifies" the Think Space for a limited number of children in our homes and professional child care environments, the actual percentage of those touched in the categories given here is small (in the one percent range). We have presented the above exclusions to both protect *children* with whom this technique should not be used as well as to protect this *technique* from failure when used with children for whom it is not designed.

CONSISTENCY

One of the keys to success in behavioral management is consistency — executing the application of a behavioral management tool in nearly the same way every time it is applied. Not that we are against variety, nor are we suggesting that our responses take on the character of a machine. What is important as the need for variation presents itself is that a parent or care provider establish a basic procedure that works well for him or her and then makes every effort to stay consistent with that procedure.

At the risk of appearing mechanical, let me assure you that children relate best to that which is familiar. The more familiar they are with the application of the Think Space, the better it will work for both child and adult.

POSITIVE DIRECTION

Using the Think Space for a child without helping him think about positive alternatives to his unacceptable behavior is a _gross violation_ of Think Space procedure!

If the Think Space is to be a useful tool in your hands, you absolutely *must* help the child think positively. Just sending the child to the Think Space with the order, "I want you to go think about what you have just done!" is far more likely to draw that child into more of the same wrong behavior than release him from it! You absolutely *must* guide him toward "using my hands to help my friends" or some such positive affirmation. (For more help with this point, refer to sections B and C in Chapter 4.)

A child will not — in fact, cannot — do this without your help so you are the key facilitator in each Think Space scenario. Thus, the *amount* of benefit a child experiences in the Think Space depends on you, his parent or care provider.

CORRECTIVE INTERACTION

As mentioned in the previous paragraph, taking a child to the Think Space without suggesting some kind of corrective interaction is another gross violation of Think Space procedure.

The personal discipline of careful correction as part of the Think Space procedure is most important. Without a few moments of personal corrective interaction between the supervising adult and the offending child, and between the offending and the offended child when appropriate, the Think Space loses at least half of its potential!

THE CHILD'S BEDROOM

General wisdom among today's best child psychologists is to avoid using the child's bedroom as the appointed destination after a reprimand. What happens when you send a child to his or her room as part of a discipline or correction scenario is that you teach the child that being near you is not acceptable when he has disappointed you and that being around you may even be unsafe!

Unless the above is actually true, *especially in the case of children below school age,* you want to have the child stay in your field of vision while in the Think Space so that you can make sure your child is spending some quality thought time there without being distracted with other things to do.

So far as the bedroom is concerned, try to keep that space associated with happy, productive activities (games, homework, creative crafts, etc.), personal activities (dressing, changing clothes, taking care of one's body, etc.) or the activities of sleeping (story telling, praying, discussing the day's events, etc.).

Enhancement B

Transferring Stress
to the Think Space

One of the purposes of the Think Space is to act as a neutralizer of the stress you endure when you do *not* use this alternative. When a child seems bent on your emotional destruction, what do you do with your stress?

An "S.O.S." call from one of our workers helped us to clarify the stress transfer principle.

"Come home quick before I strangle this kid," she said jokingly. *"He's spent most of the morning in the Think Space,"* she complained about Eric, one of her more trying charges, *"and his behavior hasn't changed a bit!"*

So, what went wrong? Did the Think Space fail to work or did she fail to work the Think Space?

First, let's not be too quick to agree that Eric was unaffected by the Think Space. As long as our helper was using the correct procedures in placing him in that space, the child was being given time to think. Those times of reflection will eventually pay off — guaranteed!

But, what if he is just testing our helper's grasp of the Think Space? What if he is enjoying seeing her frustrated response to his antics? What if he needs the security of being watched, loved and cared for? What if his emotional energy is out of balance on that day and he really *does* need the time to re-center himself? Shall we deny him the benefits of the Think Space when he needs it the most?

And, what about our helper? Was she allowing the Think Space to be the recipient of her stress, or did she only place the boy in that space but keep her stress with her? Obviously, the latter.

When you place a child in the Think Space, it is *very* important that you also deposit your stress there. The child is safe. He's not disrupting the classroom or his siblings at the moment. He's being given a chance to change his attitude. You have saved the energy you would have spent in scolding, shouting, lecturing or hitting the child. However, since stress is an intangible, it is much more difficult to manage. You can't see it, handle it, dress it or scold it. But you know it's there. You *can* feel it, see its results and talk about it.

SO, *HOW* DO YOU PLACE *STRESS* IN THE THINK SPACE?

1. Treat every time you place a child in the Think Space as if it's the *first* time he's being put there, even if it is the "umpteenth" time for the same behavior that same day! The result: you stay cool, calm and collected, refusing to carry the baggage of the child's former behavior with you as you place the child in the Think Space — again.

2. You address the child with words such as, *"Eric, I want you to think about treating your friends with courtesy,"* or some such remark that *totally* avoids any reference to previous behavior or previous visits to the Think Space. (You avoid such references because you don't want him to think that he is succeeding in building your stress until you climax with some sort of behavior that he will enjoy seeing, regardless of the consequences he may suffer!)

3. You calmly take the child by the hand, walk to the Think Space and ask him what he is going to be thinking about. Be sure he says it in positive terms, such as *"Being kind to my friends,"* rather than, *"Not hitting my friends."*

4. You ask him to stay there and think about that for a while (recently I asked a repeat offender to *"think about it five times,"* which seemed to keep the child there long enough to have some positive effect) and when he is ready to treat his friends kindly, he may return to his activity.

5. BEFORE YOU WALK AWAY, take five seconds to mentally put your stress at Eric's feet. Now leave it there. Your stress is not a friend. You don't need it. It cannot possibly do you any good. So, why hang onto it? Let the Think Space be the keeper of your stress by doing its work in the child.

6. Reassure yourself that more good is going to happen in the child this way than would come by using the alternatives — scolding, shouting or spanking — even if the results are in very small increments. But, rest assured that every time a child visits the Think Space, something positive is happening in the child. And, even though you may not be able to see it right now, eventually that inner growth will be large enough to notice.

7. Think of it as you would any developmental process — learning to play the piano, for example. Comparing your ability of today against yesterday, there will be very little discernible difference. But, if compared against your abilities of a year ago, you can tell a big difference (hopefully!).

8. Mentally, pick up your "new lease" — be sure it's the low-stress lease and not the high-stress burden you have already laid at your Eric's feet — and return to your work with your "new lease" firmly in place and in operation!

WHAT ABOUT THE NEXT TIME?

Obviously, every time your "Eric" comes out of the Think Space only to return to the same behavior again, your stress control is going to be challenged. So, what do you do? The same thing!

Why? Because repetition of the right thing is essential to the learning process. Repetition reinforces learning. As long as you are going through the procedures correctly, repetition will produce positive growth. Think of this process as a learned skill. If the Think Space isn't working for you the way it is supposed to work, you may need to give your skills more intentional scrutiny!

Check your procedures. Follow them diligently. Ask a friend to watch you and tell you what he or she is seeing. If you still need help, get in touch with us. (See the last page of Chapter 7.) We want you to experience the stress relief that you need, so let's work at it until you succeed!

Enhancement C

Using the Think Space With Older Children

CHILDREN WHO HAVE GROWN UP WITH THIS APPROACH

When a child grows up with the Think Space, it is a very normal thing to ask a school-age child to visit the Think Space for a while. By that time he will have learned to respect the idea and knows he will benefit from time spent there. We have had people report success with children as old as junior high. Even high schoolers will benefit from some time away from the immediate stresses of whatever conflict is being presently experienced.

The big change as children grow older will be for the parent or supervising adult to move away from *physically placing* a child in the Think Space to *asking* the child to spend time there and then move on to *suggesting* that he visit the Think Space. Also, the location for the Think Space will gradually shift from being in the presence or vision of the responsible adult to a more private area which may even include the child's bedroom as he moves through adolescence.

CHILDREN WHO HAVE NOT GROWN UP
WITH THIS APPROACH

Introducing the Think Space to a child who has no experience with this technique requires some explanation and discussion beforehand. Be sure to hold this conversation at a time when things are fine between you — a time when he hasn't done anything wrong in the immediate past. Say something like this:

"Tommy, I would like to suggest an idea for times when you and I have a disagreement."

Pause for his response.

"Here's the idea. Let's agree on a place where you can go to think about whatever is a problem at the moment. As long as you are there, I won't bother you. The only rule is that you may leave the Think Space when you are ready to talk with me. That will give both of us some time to think about "whatever" and should keep us from acting badly toward each other. What do you think?"

If he agrees, you're on your way to an improved relationship with your son.

If he says,

"Nah. I don't think it will work," let your response be,

"It may not work, Tommy, but I'd like to try it for, say, a month. What do you think?"

If he rejects that idea, try to negotiate a two-week trial period, one week, three days, one day and finally, "the next time." By this time Tommy will sense that you really want to give this approach a try and will probably agree to it just to stop the negotiation!

If you are unable to work out anything right then, approach the idea the next week and the next. I can guarantee that patience and persistence will finally pay off.

However, when you do finally get Tommy to cooperate, be sure to keep your end of the bargain. Absolutely discipline yourself to keep off his case while he is in the Think Space and then make the discussion afterward calm and rational. If you should fail to hold up your end of the arrangement, it may be a long time before you have that opportunity again!

While the Think Space can become a useful tool for use with many older children who have not grown up with it, here's an important fact to keep in mind: the older child who sees it being used with her younger sibling(s) may have attached to the Think Space the idea that it is for "little kids" only. If that is the case, your older child will let you know how she feels in no uncertain terms!

If and when that happens, the better part of wisdom is probably to just drop the idea, for now you are dealing with self-image which is a far more important issue than insisting on the use of the Think Space for that older child.

. . . AND SHE DID!

In closing, let me share a conversation with you between myself and a school teacher whose son was a student in our school. After I explained the Think Space to her and how it was working with her son, she gave an understanding smile and offered this comment:

"I can see how this is a great technique to use with my son. Not only are you teaching him to take some time away from whatever is bothering him, you are giving him a self-quieting tool for his future. I can see that if he were to keep up that practice as an adult, he would be able to handle his frustrations in a very responsible way."

Then she closed her affirmations with, "And you know what? I think that I could use the Think Space myself at times!"

Guess what . . .

A few days later, when she was upset over something at home, her son offered a piece of wisdom that she will never forget.

"Mommie," interrupted the five-year-old, *"I think you should spend some time in the Think Space!"*

And she did!

Enhancement D

What do you do with . . .
The Child Who "Won't" Stay
In the Think Space?

What do we do about a strong-willed child who just refuses to cooperate?

First, we must say that the child who absolutely refuses to use the Think Space is rare. The premise is this: a child will use the Think Space — at least give it a try — when it is introduced to her in an unemotional, non-threatening way.

Granted, it may not always be easy. In fact, sometimes you have to reach way down into the bottom of your creativity chest, but you will find the answer when you search for it with total determination. Here are a few techniques that have been successful for us.

To begin, **be sure you have clearly stated what you want the child to do.** Even if you have to talk through the child's emotional noises (crying, screaming, whining), when you have placed the child in the Think Space, clearly and unemotionally say,

"Sarah, you may finish this behavior here," or

"I want you to stay here until you're finished with this behavior."

If Sarah resists staying in the Think Space, try the following options, preferably in the order listed here:

a. Apply **The Three-Step Quiz:**

1. *"What did I ask* (not 'tell') *you to do?"*

2. *"What does that mean?"*

3. *"What are you going to do?"*

This little exercise, although disarmingly simple, has a really high success record with us. The key to its success is getting the child to verbalize the instruction. Once she does that, she obligates herself to respond to her own voice! Try it. You'll be amazed!

b. If Sarah still refuses to cooperate, don't force the issue right now. Rather, **let her return to her former environment**. Have no doubts. You will soon have another chance to offer the Think Space to her!

An extremely important point here, however, is to avoid "painting yourself into a corner" with comments such as:

"You're going to stay here or else," or

"You're going to stay here if it's the last thing you do,"

. . . or any such threatening verbalization. Such words clearly invite a contest, a contest that your child will probably win!

Then what happens to your credibility? It is simply erased, at least for the moment!

c. As other children visit the Think Space, if things are going well, **point out the child in the Think Space** to Sarah with words such as,

"Look, Sarah. See how nicely Eric is using the Think Space?"

It is best to do this several times before you make another attempt at helping Sarah visit the Think Space.

Then, when you *do* take Sarah there again, call to her memory the positive examples of the other children she has seen cooperating in the Think Space.

d. If Sarah is still resisting the Think Space, after you place her there, **stay with her until she settles down** — even a little bit. Remember, however, to pay as little attention to her as possible, since you are already compromising the impact of this exercise by staying with the child.

Do you recall the mother in the opening paragraphs of this book? She had to stay with the child because of the public nature of the environment and the exercise still worked for her. It can work for you, too, even if you need to stay with Sarah!

THE POINT . . . TO CALL THE CHILD'S BLUFF!

The point of this last exercise (and you will probably need to use this procedure only a few times) is simply to call the child's bluff. Remember, you are staying with the child to help her understand that you really do expect her to stay there. Furthermore, in staying with her, you also alleviate possible fears of abandonment.

Then, just as soon as any progress at all is made, quickly remove the child from the Think Space with happy affirmations and kind compliments. You may even have to compromise your own standard of readiness a bit, but a small positive start is infinitely better than no start at all!

After your first success with your "Sarah", each succeeding visit to the Think Space will be easier and more beneficial than the time before.

Enhancement E

Using the Think Space in Public

Remember the mother and child in the opening illustration of this book? I see parents every day in stores and other public places to whom I would love to show a video of that incident.

Taking the kids with you into public places can be — and often is — traumatic for both parents and care providers. But it doesn't need to be that way.

HERE'S THE PLAN!

On occasion I will take several of our students with me to the grocery store, but rarely have any problem at all because I clearly state the rules before we leave the car:

1. I will do the shopping. Any request from a child for something from the store shelves will be an automatic "no" unless I offer a choice or the item is on my shopping list.

2. Any whining or fussing will temporarily stop our shopping project. I leave my partially-loaded shopping cart with a checker while we go to the car or some other appropriate location to finish the unacceptable behavior. Then we return to finish our shopping project.

3. Anyone using poor behavior during our trip (fussing, whining, touching things, begging for "stuff") will need to stay home the next time we go shopping.

And that is the basic plan I would suggest to anyone who takes their kids shopping. Shopping can be a really good experience for kids. The secret to making shopping a positive experience for the parent or provider is to set out the rules before leaving the car or van so that the children know exactly what is expected of them and what will be the consequences of breaking the agreement or rules.

OTHER CONSIDERATIONS

Some other considerations for the use of the Think Space technique in public:

1. Be sure to **honor the plan** you have spelled out to your children. If you fail to follow through, don't blame me! I can tell you ahead of time that life with the kids will get tougher with each failure to follow through on an announced plan for behavior management.

2. Be **quick and decisive** with your response to inappropriate behavior. Avoid threats. Allow only one gentle warning. Then make your move. The longer you wait, the more difficulty you are encouraging down the road. So make your choice: either handle the situation right away and relax

the rest of the time in the store or prepare to be "up tight" the rest of the time! The ball is in your court!

3. You need to **wear a thick skin** with regard to embarrassment in public. The first moments of a Think Space exercise are usually not fun (although they may be funny from an observer's point of view). Be assured, however, that anyone who is even half alert to the ways of children will admire your quiet and decisive but non-violent response to your children's irresponsible behavior in public. Children instinctively know (or, at least, think that they know) that they can get away with more in public than they can at home because their parents and care providers don't want to embarrass themselves by having to deal with their children's poor behavior in front of other people.

4. Well, here's your chance to **call their bluff**. The mother at the restaurant refused to be intimidated by her child as he "wore out" his temper tantrum. The tantrum is the only thing that got worn out in that case because the mother flatly refused to let it affect her. In the end, they both won because Mom did the right thing, even if it was in public, and she did us all the favor of taking the noise where it would not bother the other diners in the restaurant.

5. Be on the **lookout for good Think Spaces** when you go into public with your child or children. Since children are so intuitive, your mental preparation will serve notice to them on a subliminal level which will result in their using better — maybe even their best — behavior!

6. A final key about using the Think Space in public places, however, is to avoid taking children with you when you absolutely could not take the time for a Think Space

scenario if the need should arise. Therefore, **plan your time so that you could take the extra moments if the need arises.** You'll be surprised at how much more satisfying your life with your kids will become!

Enhancement F

Key Words: "Use" - "Ready" - "Want"
"Bad" - "Can" - "Can't"

*H*ere are three very important words that you should start using right away with your children, and here's why:

"USE"

Do any of these sound familiar?

"The devil made me do it."

"You're fussing because you're tired (or hungry, or thirsty, etc.), aren't you, honey?"

"Kids, stop that fighting before I turn off the TV!"

In each case, poor behavior is being blamed on something external as if someone or something else is responsible for the way the child is behaving. This is extremely common, yet it almost always falls short of the mark. One of the inherent weaknesses of the human condition which dates clear back to the Garden of Eden ("The woman you gave me made me eat the

----

forbidden fruit!" Genesis 3:12) is our unwillingness to accept responsibility for our own choices. We're always looking for a scapegoat . . . and often succeed in finding one, usually in the form of another human who messed up our good intentions!

Actually, our resistance to taking responsibility for our own behavior and our own choices is at the root of much of the evil that plagues our world. In the presence of that mentality, personal improvement is impossible. In fact, the opposite is more likely — the worse things get, the worse things get!

In the world of adults, it is the exception who says, "I made a poor choice and now I am setting out to correct the consequences of that choice."

When we apply the word *"use"* to behavior, we make a very strategic implication — that a person has chosen, whether consciously or unconsciously, to apply certain behavior in a given situation and that he is, therefore, responsible for that choice. No one *made* him use that behavior. He is solely responsible for the outcome.

Obviously, an 18-month-old child will not be able to consciously follow that line of reasoning, but we *can* use a single word that from early on teaches him one of the hardest lessons that we humans are ever asked to learn. That word is *"use."*

"Jeffrey, what kind of behavior were you just using when you took that marker away from Andrew?"

"Sarah, is that kind behavior or rude behavior that you are using with Shanley?"

"Now, Kevin, I want you to use gentle behavior with that puzzle because it can tear very easily."

F: Use - Ready - Want; Bad - Can - Can't

"READY"

One of the great injustices that we adults impose on our little ones is to force them to immediately do whatever it is that we are asking of them with little or no regard to their personal readiness. When we force them to do things which they are not emotionally *ready* to do, we encourage hypocrisy, invite dishonesty and plant the seeds of rebellion.

The mission of the Think Space is to alleviate those unwelcome outcomes by providing the child time and space to *"get ready"* to do the thing that has been requested. Whether it is a change of attitude or an emotional log-jam of some kind, give the child a chance to change, just as you would appreciate the same courtesy as an adult.

The really great news is that children make the change from *resistance* to *readiness* much more quickly than adults and usually are able to make the needed adjustments in the two or three minutes they spend in the Think Space!

Several times in the text of this book (see Chapter 4), we have used the word *"ready"* without explanation. Now do you understand why we ask you to use that word when you are placing a child in the Think Space?

- *"When you are 'ready' to cooperate, you may come back to the classroom."*

- *"When you are 'ready' to change your attitude, you may come help us."*

- *"When you are 'ready' to let me help you work the computer, come get me."*

Can you imagine how much psychological trauma and damage you and I would have been spared if our supervising adults would have had the foresight and patience to guide us with the word *"ready"* when we were children?

Of course, to use that word *does* require a small investment — an investment called patience. However, that small investment will pay huge dividends in the future of that child. Just believe it!

"WANT"

You can avoid dozens of pitfalls in your relationship with children by using the words "I *want* you to . . . " (psychologists call these "I-messages")[1] when asking a child to do something.

As real, functioning humans, most children instinctively resist losing their identities to any sort of psychological trap. Unfortunately, direct orders are often perceived as exactly that — identity traps. Consequently, adults commonly get into needless tugs-of-war — will against will — with their children; wars which adults either lose by default or win by force, a true LOSE-LOSE situation!

Most of that sort of needless stress can be avoided simply by using the words, *"I want you to . . . "*

How does the simple phrase, *"I want you to . . . "* avoid the stress test of will against will?

When you say, *"Stop that pounding, Charlie!"* you have instantly set up a contest based on an impersonal absolute. Directly in proportion to Charlie's inherited strength of will, his human nature tests that which is presented as an absolute; the stronger his native willfulness, the greater will be the test.

He also instinctively resists the impersonalization of the command. As a human, Charlie is inherently relational. Commands that attempt to communicate using impersonal absolutes are instinctively resisted because Charlie would much prefer to respond to a personal request than to an impersonal command.

The alternative to the impersonal absolute command? Exactly the opposite, as in, *"Charlie, I want you to spend some time in the Think Space."*

"I want . . ." lets Charlie know that he is dealing with a person, not a machine.

"I want . . . " also lets him know that he has a choice in how he will respond to the directive, now that he is responding to a person and not a machine. In fact, his subconscious lets him know that right here is a quick way to develop personal identity — the identity that comes through his response to the person who is saying, *"I want you to . . . "*

Do you see how easy it is to change your directives to your children from impersonal absolutes to personal electives?

Now, here are three words that you should consciously avoid as you talk with your children, at least avoid them in the ways that they are commonly used with children for behavior control.

"BAD"

Not one time in this book (until now) have we used one of the most common words in the vocabularies of those who work with preschoolers. That word? *BAD*.

- *"Bad boy."*
- *"Bad behavior."*
- *"Bad idea."*
- *"Bad this — bad that."*

Why? Because almost any behavior, attitude or activity for which a preschooler is reprimanded can, in another situation, be appropriate and useful.

Why? Because the word *"bad"* forces the child to subscribe to an absolute black-and-white standard, and that can be both *unwise* and *unfair*.

Unwise, because the bad behavior of "screaming" may be a child's only link to survival; unwise because "crying" is a natural human emotion which, if suppressed, lays the foundation of hardness and bitterness in adulthood; *unwise* because "bouncing" may be a child's way of naturally activating his endocrine system.

Unfair, because a person who lives in a world of black and white is a judgmental person who constantly places himself into conflict with anyone who thinks differently from him;

unfair because "bad" is a word that requires a simple conditioned response while we need to train kids to think; *unfair* because the potential growth of that child's descriptive vocabulary is stunted. Rather:

- When you see rude behavior, call it "rude," not "bad."

- When you encounter impatience, call it impatient behavior rather than "bad."

- If your child treats you unfairly, name the behavior "unfair," not "bad."

"Bad" is a lazy person's shortcut. Name what you see by the word that makes it inappropriate — *"Timmy, that was rude!"* in the place of *"Timmy, that was bad."* Avoid the temptation to think the specific words you use don't make a lot of difference. They do, and you may have to pay a high price in the future for using poor word choices. You may, in fact, unwittingly be a contributor to your child's future misbehavior through the very words you presently use in correcting that child!

"CAN"

Here's a phrase I've heard people use when placing a child into Time-Out:

"When you can stop crying, you can join us in the classroom."

So, what's the matter with that?

The answer — the issue is not a matter of ability, now is it? Why not use the language that actually represents what you mean to say? Instead try,

The Think Space

"When you are finished crying, you may join us in the classroom."

How is that better?

First, even though, in both cases, you are giving the child the opportunity to finish an emotional trauma naturally rather than artificially, the word *"can"* in, *"When you can stop . . . "* implies that some sort of ability is in question here. But ability isn't the issue at all. The issue is readiness.

Second, the phrase, *"When you can stop crying . . . "* implies that there is something wrong with crying. Now stop a minute and think. What is the problem with crying?

A perceptive father once mused, *"It seems as if Grant sometimes needs to cry."*

Right on, Dad. Nothing could be more accurate. All of us need to cry. It's a very natural part of the human condition. In fact, the person who has ceased to cry has lost part of his humanity, which hurts everyone else in the human family!

So, even if you've used that sort of phrasing with children as long as you can remember, even though you do not mean anything negative by it, and even though you don't see any harm done so far, why continue with a phrase that inherently communicates wrong ideas?

Let's give our kids the best start possible. There are more than enough other obstacles to overcome. Why leave one that we can take away . . . *today?*

F: Use - Ready - Want; Bad - Can - Can't

"CAN'T"

Finally, we need to delete the word *"can't"* from our child management vocabulary. You've no doubt heard words like this:

- *"He's sitting by himself because he can't keep his hands to himself,"* or

- *"She's in Time-Out because she can't follow orders."*

Whether used by parents or providers, these irresponsible expressions are invariably used to shame children into some sort of repentant response. But it doesn't work. Instead we, the supposed keepers of the well being of our precious little people, wound and maim with words that irreparably undermine the confidence and self-esteem of the very ones we are trying to protect. We ignorantly "shoot in the foot" the very children in whom we invest our time and energy.

- *"Why can't you just sit still?"* Another familiar sound from the lips of a frustrated parent.

Do we need that word at all in the arena of discipline and correction? Not a single instance where that word cannot be substituted with more appropriate terminology comes to mind.

- Instead of: *"You're going to sit by yourself because you can't . . .",* let us say, *"You need to sit by yourself so you will think about keeping your hands to yourself."*

- Instead of: *"You're in Time-Out because you can't . . .",* we need to explain, *"You're in the Think Space to think about following our table rules."*

- Instead of: *"Why can't you just eat what's on your plate?",* we could say, *"I know that you can eat at least a little bit of each thing on your plate."*

The Think Space

Let us cease and desist from ignorantly undermining the vast potential of our children with the word *"can't"!* And in its place let us find — even invent — ways of affirming their abilities with words of support and encouragement.

BIBLIOGRAPHY

[1] *Parenting Young Children*, Don Dinkmeyer, Sr. Gary D. McKay. James S. Dinkmeyer. American Guidance Service, Circle Pines, MN, 1989, p 75-81.

Enhancement G

On "Coaxing" a Child

To avoid being abrupt or authoritarian with their children, parents and care providers frequently resort to the practice of "coaxing" — actually pleading with a child until he or she is convinced to do what the parent or provider is requesting.

"Come on, Stevie. It's time to go now. Stevie, I have a treat for you in the car. Stevie, come now. Lyle's coming over for dinner, and we have to get ready. Stevie, did you hear me? Come on, Stevie. Let's go."

On and on and on it goes — "ad nauseum"!

While we certainly *do* support the general practice of "being nice" to a child, we must, in the same breath, warn that *coaxing* has outcomes that are often less desirable than an adult's using authoritarian directives on the child. In which case, coaxing isn't "being nice" at all! Instead, you are handing a form of control to that child which is neither timely nor healthy at that point in his life. In the end, you inadvertently encourage the child to develop and perfect techniques of procrastination, avoidance of responsibility, tacit disobedience and blatant disrespect.

Think about it. Are those really the lessons you want your child to learn? I don't think so.

Of course, we are *not* condoning either coaxing or abrupt authoritarianism.

What we *are* supporting is taking initiative with a child to help him center attention on the request or directive of his adult supervisor. When Daddy says, *"Come on, now, Stevie. Let's go home,"* and Stevie resists or ignores the instruction, Daddy has a very good alternative at his disposal which he should use without delay. That option? You guessed it — the Think Space.

HELP YOUR CHILD GET READY

First, however, allow us to suggest an extremely effective technique that dates back to my mother. Instead of abruptly cutting off whatever it was that we kids were doing (homework, playing games, doing chores, etc.), she would say, *"Kids, in ten minutes it will be time to go to bed."* In that way, she helped us to prepare ourselves to do *what* she wanted *when* she wanted it done.

We have suggested the same idea to parents whose children tend to not be ready to go home when they come to pick them up. *"Try giving them a specific number of minutes,"* Carolyn will say, *"and then see what happens."* Almost without fail that simple technique solves the whole problem!

There are times, however, when advance notice does *not* do the trick. For those instances, we suggest the Think Space.

DECISIVE ACTION WITHOUT THREATS

When you have already given Stevie notice that you will be leaving in three minutes, and when Stevie fails to cooperate, you first make sure you have his full attention and then say,

"Stevie, I guess you need to go to the Think Space until you are ready to cooperate."

You say that *just once* and immediately begin to take him to the designated spot *without any other cajoling, threats, warnings.* At that point, he will probably indicate that he is ready to leave. But, if he still resists or ignores you, continue on toward the Think Space. When you get there, you say,

"I want you to stay here until you are ready to cooperate with me."

Then you walk away to another part of the room or area until Stevie is "ready."

If he tries to follow you, you may stay with him until you discern that he is either ready to stay there or is finished with his pouting. You ask,

"Are you ready now?"

If he is still whining or crying, you say,

"I'm sorry, Stevie. You aren't ready yet. I want you to finish fussing first. Then we can go home."

The strategy in this whole exercise is to reverse your position with the child from being on the *defensive* to being on the *offensive.* When you stoop to coaxing a child, you assume a *defensive* posture, a position which you can ill afford if you expect to be an effective parent or care giver. When you take the steps recommended here, you immediately move from a *defensive* position to an *offensive* position.

A QUICK AND PAINLESS TURNAROUND

A parent or care provider in a defensive position is a pitiful sight. It is our mission to help you to turn that situation around! For us and for many others, the most useful tool we have ever found to eliminate "coaxing" and to accomplish a quick and painless turnaround from a defensive to an offensive posture is the Think Space!

Enhancement H

Threats, Warnings and Counting

Sooner or later, every parent and care provider experiences the frustration of asking (or telling) a child to do something, only to be ignored — even defied. You find yourself "between the devil and the deep blue sea." If you *don't* follow through, the child has called your bluff, but if you *do* follow through, the child has succeeded in forcing you into some kind of extra effort on his behalf! So, what to do?

- Threaten? *"Johnny, if you don't come here right now, I'm going to make you wish you had!"*

- Warn? *"Johnny, remember what happened last time I had to come get you?"*

- Count? *"One . . . two . . . three . . . ."*

THREATS

When you try to motivate a child to action with the promise of some action on your part that will be undesirable to the child, you are using a threat. If you would really think about what you are doing in those cases, you probably wouldn't do it at all. But it's just so natural; it happens before you even think about it. And when it does, you've set up an inescapable trap for yourself. You either have to respond with some action that will probably not be the best for either of you, or you will let it slide, which can only make matters worse in the future — another LOSE-LOSE situation!

Most unfortunate of all, we've even seen parents use the Think Space as the object of a threat!

- *"Andrew, if you don't come right now, you're going to have to go to the Think Space!"*

- *"Boys, stop that fighting right now before I have to put you both in the Think Space!"*

You must avoid that temptation at all costs, for in so doing, you are casting the Think Space into the negative company of lectures, scolding, shouts, swats and other questionable punishments.

WARNINGS

A warning is different, both in word and in spirit, than the threat. The threat normally begins with the words "If you don't . . ." and continues with some specific consequence.

On the other hand, a warning tends to be more indirect, as in,

- *"Am I going to have to . . . ?"*, or

- *"Do you remember what happened . . . ?"*

A warning is also usually framed in a kinder, gentler spirit than is the threat. It is a parent or care giver's way of threatening action without the negativity generally associated with the threat.

H: Threats, Warnings and Counting

A warning is less likely to arouse rebellion than the direct threat and is often successful in motivating children to improve their behavior without physically abusive alternatives.

However, a warning still teaches the child that he needs to give serious attention to whatever request has been made *only after a warning follows the original command.*

COUNTING

We don't know who first came up with the counting alternative, but we used it with our children. We learned it from someone else older than ourselves. And our children have used the practice with their children.

While counting does give the child some time to respond to your command, it also teaches the child to wait until a certain magic number before he honors your request. Now think. Is that what you want from your child? No? Then why do you continue that practice?

If what we have just pointed out isn't enough, think of this: if you are a counter, just what is your magic number? Of course, the child knows that something unpleasant is likely to happen when you get to three or ten or any other number that you tend to use as the last number. But do *you* know what will happen when you get to the magic number when you *start* counting?

Here's the problem. If, at the start of your counting, you don't already know what you are going to do when you reach the magic number, you put yourself and your child into a position of your having to do something — anything — just to carry through with the threat you have started. The sad fact is that what you do at the end of your counting will probably *not* be in the best interest of either you or the child. Such situations can easily lead to ill-advised actions that are both thoughtless and destructive.

CREDIBILITY UP FOR GRABS!

The most difficult thing about threats and warnings is the fact that every time you use that kind of device as a motivational technique, you are putting your credibility on the line. In other words, if you don't follow through with some kind of unpleasant response, you have allowed the child to undermine your credibility (the degree to which he can believe in you). And, since the subconscious mind does not distinguish between negative and positive ideas, from the child's perspective, you are truly undermining the believability of *both* your negative <u>and</u> your positive instruction.

SO, WHAT SHALL WE DO?

A wise man once quipped,

"If you keep on doing what you've always done, you'll keep on getting what you've always gotten!"

In other words, if you don't like what you see in your child's responses to your requests, make the necessary adjustments to get the results you want!

NO FURTHER EVIDENCE NEEDED!

Look! The very fact that your child has chosen to either ignore or defy you should already tell you that he needs some extra thinking time. *You need no further evidence or notice.* In such cases you should immediately, and without any threat or warning, calmly but firmly take the child to the Think Space. (We're assuming that you will give appropriate thinking instructions while in the Think Space as detailed in the earlier chapters of this book.)

To use any kind of motivation other than your simple request, is to complicate your life — and his — with more of the very thing that you are wanting to overcome! **In other words, every time you use a threat or warning, you are teaching the child that he doesn't actually need to respond until you do or say something else, something more emphatic.**

Even more damaging is the negativity you unwittingly model in those situations. You unconsciously teach leadership by negativity, a trait that he will most certainly copy. You have stooped to rule by fear rather than by respect. You have set up a parent-child response cycle that is very difficult to break.

A TIME FOR CHANGE!

So, if you find yourself using *threats*, you need to consciously discipline yourself against continuing with that practice.

If your motivational technique is more along the *warning* line, you still need to look carefully at the logical outcome of that practice.

If you are given to *counting*, it may work now, but what are you teaching? Better to forget you ever learned to count!

If you are a user of any of these, you need to find other ways of communicating your seriousness. The Think Space is one very good alternative.

A good alternative is to go to the child before you give your command a second time, take him by the hand and help him do whatever it is you requested.

Another is to go to the child, kneel down so your face is near his, gently take his face in your hand and go through . . .

THE THREE-STEP QUIZ:

1. *"What did I ask you to do?"*

2. *"What does that mean?"*

3. *"What are you going to do?" . . . "When?"*

NEVER INTENDED TO BE A PUNISHMENT!

Here's the bottom line. **The Think Space was NEVER intended to be used as a punishment and therefore, if properly understood, would never be used as part of a threat, a warning or a counting scenario.**

Instead, it is to be used as an opportunity — an opportunity for the child to rethink his response to his parent or care provider in a less pressured environment. It is an opportunity for your child to take some extra time to come to the same decision that you have already assumed . . . and time for you to think about other ways of getting the same thing accomplished without a show-down of wills.

Finally, if you are a new parent, or hope to one day be one, you have a truly wonderful opportunity to *decide now* to simply *not* use the counterproductive practice of threats, warnings or counting . . . ever! You will find that you simply do *not* need them once you have removed them from your list of motivational options!

1

Enhancement 1

The Cry . . .
and what to do about it!

As the ultimate pragmatist, the child learns from early on how to use the ultimate motivational device — *the cry*.

At birth the human infant has but one means of communication with the new environment which has been foisted upon him — *the cry*. For nine months he has enjoyed the intimate, protective warmth of his mother's womb. Now, suddenly, he is pushed into a world which offers precious little protection or warmth. His response — *the cry*.

DID YOU HEAR THE BABY CRY?

And what is our response to *the cry?* We try to understand what the baby is wanting with one overriding objective — to stop *the cry!*

It may well be that the very first learning a baby experiences is the quick response that *the cry* brings. Immediately we seek to

----

soothe his frustrated reaction to his new, hostile surroundings, and that is the way it should be.

In fact, the development of trust between infant and parent is nourished largely by the successful satisfaction of the child's felt needs expressed through *the cry*. Researchers have convincingly shown that human development — both emotional and intellectual — is strongly impacted by the quality of the trust relationship between infant and care giver (parent).[1] Therefore, it is a mistake to allow an infant to cry without making an honest effort to alleviate its discomfort. The general rule: responding to the cry of an infant creates trust while ignoring its cry creates distrust.

A SPECIAL PLACE

Also, keep in mind that, when you *do* begin to selectively ignore certain cries, the distinguishing element that separates responsible ignoring from inadvisable ignoring is the use of a special place designated for unacceptable crying. If you ignore a child's cry without any kind of acknowledgment, the child will likely feel that you don't care about him, which damages his trust in you and slows his development as a person.

If, on the other hand, you take time to acknowledge the child's crying and then place him where crying will be okay, you assure him that you care about him, thereby preserving the trust factor while teaching that crying in certain cases is an exercise in futility!

Again, we need to emphasize that the focus of this book and the techniques it teaches are for children 18 months to school age (kindergarten). Application of these methods to children outside that age frame needs to be carried out with appropriate modifications. (For use with older children, see Enhancement C.)

NEWTON'S THIRD LAW OF MOTION

As the infant's powers of learning develop, Newton's Third Law of Motion quickly kicks in. That physical law, which states that "for every action there is an equal and opposite reaction," has a precisely parallel application in the world of children.

When a mother responds to her crying baby to give it what it *does* need, she also, inadvertently, teaches the child how to get what it *may not* need! And most children, given their natural disposition of opportunism, very soon learn to exploit their new-found power — *the cry.*

A CRUEL REALITY

It's a kind of cruel reality for both parent and child to discover that neither one knows exactly how to discern between what is actually needed and what is wanted but not necessarily needed.

What thousands of years of experience *have* taught us, however, is this: between the child's twelfth and eighteenth months, it is a good idea to begin teaching the child that he is not going to be able to totally control his adult care givers with *the cry.*

Herein lies another cruel reality. To teach an infant that his cries are not going to totally control his adult world, there will be times that he will need to cry without getting the response he wants, and he will need to do that until he is convinced that his crying is not going to be rewarded in that instance.

And, while some parents are able to ignore inappropriate cries of their children without personal trauma, some parents have a really hard time with this exercise, even though they may mentally agree with it! Regardless of how a parent responds to this part of child training, the truth is that success in this department translates into the child's ability to exercise his own inner control as he matures into adolescence and later into adulthood.

In any case, right there is the watershed between the parent who chooses to **manage** his child and the one who is **managed by** his child. That all-purpose contrivance, *the cry*, used by the child for everything from survival to mutiny, is so powerful that it requires the wisdom of a Solomon, the intelligence of an Einstein, and the emotional steadiness of a Clara Barton to understand its present purpose!

You know what we're saying is true, because you've seen the tyranny of *the cry* in action. If you haven't seen it at work in your own children, you have surely seen it in your neighbor's kids!

So, why are we adults so influenced, so controlled by *the cry?* Basically, for only two reasons: compassion and nerves.

COMPASSION

Our hearts just naturally go out to the child who cries. We instinctively want to fix "whatever" to, in some way, supply the security that birth took away. We do what we can to help that child feel better about his new environment and the people who surround him.

And that's as it should be, for it is only in such an environment of caring love that a helpless infant can survive in an otherwise hostile world.

However, our compassion can also get us into trouble, for we have a hard time exercising "tough love" on a child who can't even talk yet, much less reason with us.

One fall morning, I found Keri's mother and sister bent over her in the car as she resisted leaving them to come to her new preschool. She had them in her control. How? *The cry.*

"We're trying to reason with her," said the mother as I walked past the car.

"Sometimes there is no reasoning," I quipped, which was precisely the problem. They thought the problem was about reason while it was actually about control. The child was playing the compassion of her sister for all it was worth. Keri had her sister feeling so badly that she wanted her mother to take Keri back home!

Thankfully, in the end, the mother's wisdom prevailed. Keri spent the day with us and thoroughly enjoyed herself.

So what's the point here?

If the child had succeeded in her play for control, two things would have happened:

- She would have been given the power to make a decision for which she had neither the wisdom nor the experience,

- She would have won her power through the misuse of that nearly all-powerful device — the cry!

In both cases the success of that moment would have encouraged more of the same, which would, in turn, have made life more difficult for both mother and sister! From that day forward, the influence of both mother and sister in Keri's life would have been reduced, for they would have compromised it that day, all because of *the cry!*

NERVES!

The other reason that we are so strongly affected by a child's cry is *nerves*. The sensitivity of most adults to *the cry* of a child dictates that *the cry* has to stop, almost regardless of whatever compromises are required to stop it.

That, after all, is the purpose of *the cry*. It's loud, harsh sound is designed to get a response. Ironically, the way we adults are designed leaves us open and vulnerable to the sound of *the cry*.

So, when someone suggests that a child be allowed to cry until the child is "finished," such words can easily fall on deaf ears, if for no other reason than to avoid having to listen to *the cry*.

The trouble is that the young child, being both egocentric and opportunistic, will instinctively exploit *the cry* for his own ends. Our response to *the cry* — especially to the exploiting cry — does much to shape both the child's future and our future with that child.

Therefore, it is important for us to understand and find a way of dealing with *the cry* that is instructive rather than destructive.

A SAFE PLACE TO CRY

Of course, you know where I am going with this — yes, indeed — to the Think Space, the perfect place for crying to be "spent" without exploiting anyone.

As long as you have seen to it that the essential needs — hunger, cleanliness, security, basic health — of a child are being met, you can be fairly certain that a child's cries fall into the exploitation category. Or, perhaps your child is truly sad or emotionally out of control.

Whatever the case, there is little fear of harming a child by taking him to the "Cry Space" to "finish" crying. Plus, by placing him outside the adult's immediate area of activity to do his crying, the disruptiveness of *the cry* is reduced.

When we finally realize

- that it is okay for a child to cry,

- that it is a natural function of being human,

- that a delicate balancing mechanism for the emotional health of the child is being developed within,

- that once we get beyond the crying, our life with the child will be more pleasant,

then and only then can we accept the idea that *stopping the cry* may be the *cruel* alternative and letting it run its natural course may be the *most compassionate* option!

Finally, once you understand what's going on with *the cry*, you hear it differently, just as the nauseous belches from the trombone of a beginner are much more tolerable to the ears of his admiring parent than to the family's sleeping neighbor!

In any case, once you have figured out what *the cry* really is and how to use it to the benefit of both the child and yourself, life will be much more relaxed and infinitely more rewarding — all because you now understand *the cry*.

BIBLIOGRAPHY

[1] *Child Development and Relationships*, Carol Flake-Hobos, Bryan E. Robins, Patsy Skean. Random House, New York, 1983, p124, 146.

The Think Space

For Your Personal Notes

Parting Thoughts

the Epilogue

In evaluating the Think Space, Dr. Ed Christophersen thoughtfully observed, *"What you are doing is asking parents and providers to teach a skill to their children which they may not have yet learned for themselves (i.e., how to step back from a stressful situation to think about it before it becomes a crisis)!"*

While the Think Space was developed specifically for young children, it is actually born out of a very wise piece of advice that comes from the pen of one who wrote clear back in the first century, A.D., *"Be quick to listen, slow to speak and slow to anger."* [1]

Whatever else may be said about working with children, one thing is almost universally true: the most important discipline in child management needs to be applied, not to our children, but to **ourselves**, particularly to the areas of what we *hear* them say, what we *say* in response to them and what we do with our frustrations — our *anger*.

The Think Space

As we write the closing words of this book, two sets of our client-parents are working through their own tendencies to "lose the handle" on their emotions in working with their children at home. The irony of both situations is that neither of those children give us a dime's worth of trouble when they are with us, while they can be absolute terrors with their parents!

In both cases, we have shown those parents how important it is to make their responses to their children's emotion-arousing behaviors as uninteresting as possible.

For starters, we have shared with them the words of Dr. Vincent Barone, who offers a very relevant insight:

"I'm convinced that kids just want life to be interesting. If it isn't, they find ways to make it that way. To the delight of our children, most of us unwittingly oblige them with our responses to the behaviors that they invent for that very purpose!" [2]

In both cases, the parents of the two children mentioned earlier have made life far too interesting to their two and three-year-olds with their emotional styles of response to their children's alternative behaviors!

Now, here's the good news. After some careful, but pointed instruction, both families are experiencing increasing success in managing their children by using the Think Space (Cry Space) without emotion or other interesting behaviors on their (the parents') parts.

Of course, other disciplines must support their new-found emotional control — consistency, positive communication, using the Think Space to "finish" inappropriate behavior rather than using it as a point of punishment, and so on.

Always remember, however, that every child looks first to you, his parent or care provider, to see how life works. If he sees you respond to the crises of life (be they small or large) with disciplined calmness, he learns that is the way life works best. However, if he *sees* the opposite, he too will *use* the opposite.

Together we have spent several hours together discussing wholesome ways to manage young children. In so doing, we have prepared you to do an uncommon thing — to actually give your child the time and space to think about how life can work better.

So, while your *child* is taking time to think, why don't *you* take time to think too? In the end both you and your child will gradually develop a lifestyle of love, understanding and harmony because you have *both* discovered a wonderful new space — the Think Space!

BIBLIOGRAPHY

[1] *New American Standard Bible* (James 1:19). Holman Bible Publishers, Nashville, TN. 1984.

[2] Dr. Vincent J. Barone, Ph.D., Licensed Psychologist; Associate Professor of Pediatrics, University of Kansas Medical Center. From the seminar titled: *Successful Parenting,* presented in October, 1995, Mission, KS.

Here is your key to . . .

THE THINK SPACE

Use this key as a bookmark. After finishing the book, post this key in a prominent place to help you remember the proper use of this remarkable technique.

1. Calmly and patiently *take – never send* – your child to the Think Space.

2. Allow your child to *finish* inappropriate behavior in the Think Space without guilt or repression.

3. Help your child to *think* about how to respond the next time; i.e., help him *look forward* to better choices in the future.

4. Instruct your child to leave the Think Space when he is *finished* thinking and is *ready* to cooperate.

5. Look for a *change of attitude,* demonstrated by willing "cooperation."

6. Guide your child to *repair* damaged relationships and/ or physical property as he exits the Think Space.

(Adapted from Think Space comparison chart in Chapter 5)

Glossary of Terms
used in The Think Space

All the terms defined here are written to support the way they are used in this book and may need to be expanded or adjusted for other settings or disciplines.

Each defined term in this glossary is included in the Index which follows.

Actualization - The process of bringing something that is present in a person's mind into a form that can be seen and/or experienced by others. "Materialization" is a close synonym. The expressions "becoming real" or "becoming reality," although inaccurate, are also commonly used as synonyms of "actualization."

Attitude adjustment - A popular way of referring to the process of changing a person's way of thinking and/or speaking about or relating to a given matter; otherwise known as "a change of attitude."

Behavior modification - A term coined by behavioral scientists during the early 1900's to refer to the process of altering specific undesirable behaviors and changing them into desirable behaviors through the use of negative and positive consequences (reinforcements).

Child management - A term used throughout this book as an alternative to other more common terms (child rearing, child discipline and parenting). The reason for the change is that "child management," as we describe it, more accurately describes the role that parents and care providers should have in the lives of the children under their care.

The Think Space

Child management techniques - Planned responses by parents and adult care providers which are applied to situations that commonly and repeatedly occur in the lives of children. The Think Space is the most recent addition to a long list of techniques ranging from scolding and spanking to Time-Out.

Control - Three definitions in the *American Heritage Dictionary* describe our use of control in this book: "*tr.v.* **1.** To exercise authoritative dominating influence over; direct. **2.** To hold in restraint; check . . . *n.* **1.** Authority or ability to manage or direct . . ." In the context of this book, it is our primary goal to *control* environments but *manage* people, including children. Also, see the definition for "manager" in this glossary.

Controllers - Those who engage in the the practice of controlling as defined in "control" above.

Corrective interaction - The process of reviewing with a person his inappropriate response to a given situation with the goal of improved response to the same or similar situations.

Cry Space - An alternative name given to the Think Space when it is used by a child to "finish" his crying over a specific disappointment or frustration. Other common alternatives include "Pout Space" and "Angry Space."

Delirious emotional state - The *American Heritage Dictionary* describes "delirium" as; "*n.* **1.** A temporary state of mental confusion and clouded consciousness resulting from high fever, intoxication, shock or other causes . . . characterized by hallucinations, delusions, trembling and incoherent speech. **2.** A state of uncontrolled excitement or emotion." Our use of this term describes a condition that overtakes some children in which they lose all sense of rationality as they respond to a situation which greatly annoys or frightens them. (Admittedly, that point is subjective, since some children present the appearance of losing rationality before they actually lose it.) Once that state of delirious emotionality is reached, any benefit from behavioral techniques that are based in rationality, including the Think Space, are basically ineffective and can even be injurious to the emotional health of the child.

Diffusion - Phase Two of the three phases of the Think Space technique. In this phase, the child is given the time and space to "drain" his inappropriate behavior, which results in that behavior losing its strength or control over that child.

Emotional deposit - A process by which a child sets up emotional ownership of a geographic location by expressing a behavior in that location which he instinctively knows is unacceptable to his parent or adult care provider promoted.

Emotionally-challenged - A term given to children who have clinically-diagnosable emotional weaknesses or illnesses, whether genetically inherited or developed after birth due to unusual circumstances in those children's lives.

Emotional Intelligence - A person's ability to consciously or unconsciously control his own emotions in the circumstances of life, particularly in relation to interpersonal relationships. Although not yet reduced to standardized measurements like IQ, this part of human intelligence in children — the ability to handle frustrations, control personal emotions and get along with other people — are indicators of emotional intelligence.

EQ (Emotional Quotient) - A term used in recent research to describe the ability of a person to control his emotional disposition in real-life situations, particularly in relation to interpersonal relationships.

IQ (Intelligence Quotient) - A score obtained on a standardized test of intelligence and based on the hypothetical construct (idea) that there is a correlation between IQ and school achievement. It is a measurement of the ability of a person to perform activities of the intellect as compared with others of his same chronological age. IQ is considered to be a constant that changes little throughout the lifespan.

LowStress Child Management - An innovative child management system which features techniques and procedures in harmony with the way children think and learn, resulting in environments characterized by lower-than-average stress levels for both the child and his care providers (including parents).

The Think Space

Manager - By definition, a manager is; "*n.* **1.** One who handles, controls or directs, especially: **a.** One who directs a business or other enterprise. **b.** One who controls resources and expenditures, as of a household. . ." *(American Heritage Dictionary).* Our use of manage and manager emphasizes the directing aspect, while minimizing the controlling part of the definition. We see the manager as a person who works with that which already exists (material resources, behaviors, circumstances) to bring about conditions that do not yet exist (order, harmony, creativity). In both child-care and home environments, the manager operating style is basically the opposite of the controller style (see "control" earlier in these definitions).

Mentally-challenged children - A term given to children who have contracted clinically-diagnosable mental weaknesses or illnesses, whether genetically inherited or developed after birth due to unusual circumstances in those children's lives.

Montessori Method - The name given to the child guidance technique developed by Maria Montessori during the late 1800's and early 1900's. The system is characterized by helping children learn through their individual internal guidance systems more than by external lessons and pre-set time tables.

Newton's Third Law of Motion - Literally, "For every action there is an equal and opposite reaction." Applied to child management, the idea is that when a child does something that gets him what he needs, he also learns to get what he wants but doesn't necessarily need.

Pragmatist - A person who uses practical but usually unsophisticated ways of approaching situations and solving problems. The ultimate pragmatist is the child, for he experiments until he finds a way to get what he wants and then simply repeats, without conscious calculation or intentional reasoning, the same technique when similar situations present themselves.

Psyche - Generally defined as the spirit or soul. In psychiatry, it is regarded as the mind functioning as the center of thought, emotion, and behavior. The conscious part (the ego) and the unconscious part (the id) work together to adjust a person's responses to his social and physical environment. (From the *American Heritage Dictionary*)

Reality checks - A popular way to express the process of looking honestly at a condition or circumstance in life and see it for what it really is rather than seeing in it only what we want to see.

Resolution - Step Three in the operation of the Think Space in which the child makes amends with whoever was the object of offense or whatever was damaged in the unacceptable behavioral scenario from which he has earlier been separated.

Self-quieting skills - Abilities that the child can use to help himself calm down after an emotional upset; abilities which should result from the proper application of the Think Space.

Separation - Step One in the operation of the Think Space in which the child is physically removed from the scene of an unacceptable behavioral scenario.

Stress transfer principle - The notion that a person can emotionally remove a specific stress from himself and transfer it to another place, person or thing. In reality, it is a procedure in which responsibility for the outcome of a particular situation is removed from a person to another person, place or thing, thus removing the stress connected with that circumstance.

Teachable moment - An educational term used to describe particular times in a person's life in which various understandings merge with the result that some lesson or idea that formerly was misunderstood or not understood at all, now is clearly understood.

Think Space - A behavior management technique developed for use with preschool children which uses the same scientific base as the Time-Out technique (see definition in this glossary), i.e., removing a child from an environment to quiet himself. Some of the distinctives of the Think Space which distinguish it from Time-Out include; 1) the child being encouraged to use the Think Space to "finish" behavior which is unacceptable in another setting, 2) the adult care provider guiding the child to think about improved behavior in the future while in the Think Space, and 3) the control of leaving the Think Space being shared by both the child and the adult care provider.

The Think Space

Three-Choice Quiz - A series of three questions that help a child to focus on three ideas: a) whatever responses he uses as situations come along are choices that he personally makes, and b) which one of the three choices he actually used and c) which choice would be a better alternative the next time that same kind of situation comes along. The three choices are 1) to fuss, 2) to ignore and 3) to work it out.

Three-Step Quiz - A series of three questions that help a child to focus on some request that a parent or care provider has made of a child but is not being performed. The three questions of this procedure are 1) "What did I ask you to do?" 2) "What does that mean?" and, 3) "What are you going to do?" The effectiveness of this procedure comes from the fact that, when the child answers all three questions correctly, he has repeated the same request three times in his own words and with his own lips, thereby producing an inner motivation (actually, a compelling obligation) to do as requested.

Time-Out - A behavioral management technique first developed for use with autistic children and later for normal children. This technique removes a child from an environment in which he is using inappropriate behavior to allow that child to quiet himself and to later return to his former environment in a more sociable frame of mind.

Validation - A term that basically means "to establish the soundness of, to corroborate, to confirm, to authenticate" a particular experience or point of view. We adults "validate" the power of many behaviors used by children in the ways that we respond to them, particularly to unacceptable behaviors. As mentioned in the text, the more attention we give to a selected behavior with traditional methods, the more we validate its strength and, concurrently, the strength of the child using that behavior.

Visualization - The practice of mentally picturing or imagining a particular idea as the first step in the materialization or actualization of that idea. The Think Space uses visualization in step two of the complete cycle, named Diffusion. In this step the child is helped to think about (visualize) how he will handle that or a similar situation the next time it presents itself.

Index

of key words used in The Think Space

The Think Space

Order Form

✉ Mail orders: Complete form below
✳ Fax orders:* Toll-free: 1-888-22THINK (228-4465)
☎ Telephone orders:* Toll-free: 1-888-44THINK (448-4465)
  *Credit Card orders only

Please send _____ copies of **THE THINK SPACE** to:

NAME: _____

COMPANY NAME: _____

ADDRESS: _____

CITY: _____ ST: _____ ZIP:_____

PHONE(S): _____

PAYMENT INFORMATION
Price Per Copy $14.95

NUMBER OF COPIES ORDERED (___ x 14.95)
Shipping & Handling:
Surface mail: first book: $2.00 (3-4 weeks delivery)   _____
        Additional books to same address: $1.00 ea.   _____
Priority mail: $3.50 per book (x) _____ (1 week delivery)   _____
SUB TOTAL   _____
Sales tax:
        Add 4.9% for books shipped to Kansas addresses   _____
TOTAL PAYMENT   _____

Payment:
  ❑ Check # _____   ❑ Money Order # _____
    (Make check or M.O. payable to *"Take V Publications"*)
  Credit card: ❑ VISA   ❑ MasterCard
    Card # _____
    Name on Card: _____
    Expiration Date: _____

Send order and payment to: **Take V Publications**
                            P.O. Box 4490
                            Overland Park KS 66204-4490

Call toll-free and order today!
- - - - - - - - - - - - - *1 (888) 44THINK (448-4465)* - - - - - - - - - - - - -

*Calvin and/or Carolyn Richert are available for lectures, workshops,
seminars, etc. You may contact them at 1-913-341-9550.*

(Separate order form from book along perforated line.)